The Muffin Baker's Guide

by Bruce Koffler

illustrated by Clive Dobson

Firefly Books

© Firefly Books Ltd., 1983
All rights reserved.
Second edition (revised) 1984
Fifth printing, 1989
isbn 0-920668024-0

acknowledgement:
My thanks to the Winter family in Cumberland, Ontario —
Linda, Mike, Sean, Chris and Andy. They tasted and
passed judgement on many hundreds of muffins during
the two years required to prepare this book.

Firefly Books Ltd.
250 Sparks Avenue
Willowdale, Ontario, Canada
M2H 2S4

Printed in Canada

Contents

Basic and Bran Muffins

Baking Tips for Muffins

1. Many people prefer to use *honey* instead of sugar. Chemically, they are identical, but if you prefer to substitute honey for sugar in a recipe which calls for sugar, it is wise to *halve* the quantity required. Recipes which have been formulated and tested with sugar have a different moisture-to-flour balance. Adding too much honey throws the liquid balance off and may result in muffins that are soggy, do not rise properly, or have other unwanted characteristics. Sugar in some recipes also acts to stiffen the batter when baked. By adding honey in some recipes and reducing the sugar, you may also have to reduce the egg or milk. If you do not mind wasting $2 or $3 in ingredients by trying substitutions, then, by all means, experiment. Not all experimentation will result in failure. The results may be better, or preferred to the recipe as written here.

2. *Baking soda* is chemically different from *baking powder*. Baking soda is usually used only in mixtures which have acidic ingredients in addition to the non-acidic ones. Use of baking soda allows a slight reduction in the amount of baking powder, which some find gives a faintly objectionable taste. Double acting baking powder contains some baking powder and some baking soda. It is currently available as a "no-name" product.

3. Some types of *seeds*, such as sunflower seeds, can be home-ground to make a coarse meal using a coffee bean mill, or may be bought in that form in health food stores. Some seeds are better used in a recipe as meal, rather than as flour or as whole seeds.

4. *Milk* in some recipes is specified as *sour* milk. This is used with baking soda to produce the rising of the batter and also imparts a slightly sour flavor which is desirable with some recipes. If sour milk is not at hand, regular milk may be instantly soured by the addition of a little vinegar to it, or a little lemon juice. Add one or the other to the milk at the rate of 1 tablespoon to 1 cup of milk.

5. *Nuts* give muffins crunch and flavor. To ensure crunchiness, nuts should not be added to any liquid part of the recipe (oil, milk, eggs, water), or they will soak up the liquid and become soggy. Nuts will sink to the bottom of batter if they are not first "floured". Flouring means thoroughly coating a solid ingredient, such as nuts or fruits, by stirring it around in flour. Some nuts have a very strong flavor and should be used in moderation. In some recipes you may increase the amount of nuts by ⅓ to ½ more than are

called for. If you overdo it, however, the muffin may be too crunchy, as nuts alter the texture of batter. Walnuts and filberts, especially, cause this problem if too many are added. Whole nuts make the muffin too lumpy. At the same time, if nuts are chopped too fine they will impart flavor but too little crunch — they'll get lost in the batter.

6. *Butter* is usually termed "sweet" or "salted". Sweet or unsalted butter is the natural product derived directly from cream. Salted butter is sweet, creamery butter with salt added. Recipes which call for butter should be assumed to require *sweet* butter, and usually call for some amount of salt to be included in the list of ingredients. If you use salted butter, then adding the amount of salt called for in the recipe's list of ingredients may give the muffins an excessively salty taste. In almost every case, you can make the muffins with sweet butter and leave out the amount of salt called for without making them taste "bad". Persons on salt-free or salt-reduced diets do not need to fear leaving out the salt and having the recipe flop. They should also be aware that chemicals used in the leavening agents (baking powder, baking soda), have a sodium component, and that some recipes call for a large amount of leavening. If you have a health problem related to sodium intake, there are some recipes which require very little or no baking powder. Try the others only on your physician's advice.

7. *Shortening* may occasionally replace butter or oil content of a recipe. You can substitute shortening in equal amount to butter which the recipe calls for. Shortening is not a pure oil, nor is butter. Both contain about equal amounts of water (moisture) and that is why equal amounts can be substituted. *Oils*, however, have no water in them, being pure fat. If you are using butter or vegetable shortening in place of vegetable oil, use about ⅓ cup butter for each ¼ cup oil called for in the recipe. ¼ cup oil is a common measure used in many muffin recipes. The reason for using a little more butter, or shortening, is that if the recipe calls for a specific amount of fat, it is best to use that amount. As butter is 20 percent or more water, which boils away in the baking process, your recipe is "starved" for fat and not as tender. Your muffins may taste too dry, may be crumbly or otherwise unpalatable if improper substitution is made. Excessive substitution makes the muffins too greasy. Your muffins should not leave a greasy residue on your fingers. Nut oils may burn or otherwise change flavor during baking of muffins especially in recipes calling for a hot oven (400° to 425°F) and should not be used.

8. *Eggs* add a portion of the liquid requirement of the recipe and also

provide some of the flavor. The baking process also cooks the protein, which acts to support or stiffen flour and prevent collapse of the muffin. Beating eggs mixes air into the liquid. This air expands when heated in the oven, and acts to leaven or lighten muffins. In doing this, beaten egg helps make the muffin rise. Some recipes call for the egg to be "separated". This means that the white is removed from the yolk and dealt with separately. The way to do this is to crack the egg slightly, and work your finger nails between the two halves of the cracked shell. *Slowly* force the 2 halves apart, over a bowl, and the white will begin to ooze from the shell, flowing into the bowl. You must exert some control over the shell halves to keep the yolk from slipping past. There may still be some white left in the shell. Close the shell, tilt it, and then slowly reopen the halves. The remaining white should flow into the bowl. It does not matter if a *very small* amount of white remains with the yolk. Once you have separated the two components, treat them as called for in the recipe. "Eggs beaten separately" means this component separation is made first. It does *not* mean that you take two eggs and beat them in different bowls!

9. *Milk substitute* can be made for use by persons on dairy-free diets. For each cup of milk required by the recipe, substitute 1 cup of water mixed with 1 tablespoon of lemon juice and ½ teaspoon of baking soda.

10. *Flour* varies in the amount of moisture it contains, depending on day-to-day environmental humidity, conditions of storage, type of flour used and elevation of your location above sea level. Therefore, you may sometimes find that the recipe as presented in this book may turn out a little too dry or a little too moist for your taste. The next time you make the recipe, try it with a *little* more or less water or milk, using a tablespoon as a standard measure. If the muffins were a little too moist, reduce the liquid by a tablespoon next time, if all other factors are the same, to see if this gives a slightly drier result. Flour stored in its original bag will absorb moisture from the air on humid days, and may cake up, be lumpy, or settle in the measuring cup and pack tighter. When such flour is used, I recommend that it be sifted before measuring to get a more accurate measurement. Flour can be less subject to changes in humidity (and infestations by insects), if it is stored in a glass jar with a wide mouth.

11. *Oven temperatures* shown are indicated for the standard electric oven, preheated to the temperature shown. This varies for different recipes, depending on the amount of liquid and the size of the individual muffin cups. Both Fahrenheit and Celsius reading

4

are shown. You will note that generally, with lower temperatures, a longer baking time (usually 10 to 15 minutes more) is required. An oven is in most cases hotter at the top than at the bottom, but will depend on the electrical elements — top and bottom — used to produce heat. Temperatures can vary 25° to 30° in different parts of the oven, which is why I suggest placement on a centre shelf as standard procedure. In addition, and unknown to you, your thermostat may be giving a false reading by 25° to 50°, which will affect your recipes. If you try a number of recipes and they do not work out, place an oven thermometer in the oven to see if your stove setting is accurate — too high, too low or just right. Oven thermometers are available at hardware stores and kitchen utensil sections of department stores.

12. *Microwave Ovens* can be used to bake muffins, but the technique, equipment used and finished product all vary from those used in electric or gas oven baking. Microwaved muffins require a shorter baking time, but this depends on the number of muffins made in one batch. Also, the quantity of batter poured into each cup is reduced to ½ (rather than the usual ⅔ or ¾ cup) as microwave oven-made muffins usually double in volume. *You cannot use aluminum muffin tins in a microwave.* A special "cupcaker" assures good shape and even cooking for muffins and cupcakes. It is a disk with 6 holes, into which you place either cupcake paper liners, or the lower 1-inch section of cut-down hot drink paper cups, with a paper cupcake liner inside. This hot-drink cup arrangement can also be used with a flat plate (microwave oven-proof). Arrange the cut-down paper cups, with cupcake liners, in a circle on the plate. The cups should also be rotated ½ turn halfway through the baking time to ensure even baking through the batter. With a microwave, the muffins will appear barely set after minimum baking time, and may have moist spots on top. Test by inserting a wooden toothpick into the centre of each muffin. It should come out clean, with no batter clinging to it. The muffins made in a microwave oven *will not brown*, and so it is advisable to use a recipe with colored ingredients, or use one of several toppings to add color. (Ovens with a convection setting will brown the muffins.)

13. *Sugar* as generally used in these recipes means white granulated sugar. If you substitute brown for white sugar, the results may change due to higher moisture content of brown sugar.

14. Storage of muffins which are not eaten immediately, should be in a container loosely covered with a cloth. If you store muffins in a glass jar or cookie tin with a tightly-fitting top, they will get a moist and sticky coating on the outside. Don't leave a glass jar of muffins in a sunny window.

15. To produce higher-rising muffins, pre-heat the greased muffin tin in the oven. Then spoon the batter into the pre-heated tin while it is still resting on the partly-removed oven shelf. Don't set the hot tin on your table top or plastic counter!

16. PAM® spray can be used as a convenient replacment for butter or shortening to grease the muffin tins.

17. With some recipes, you may try first beating the egg alone, until it becomes frothy, *then* add the oil and other liquids and continue beating. This tends to reduce splashing of liquids onto walls and clothing!

18. Remove butter, milk and eggs from the refrigerator half an hour before using them in any recipe and let them warm up on the counter.

Basic Muffins*

This recipe is used to bake an ordinary, unadorned muffin, which is best served hot, with a pat of butter melting in. A number of recipes follow this one, which are variations on the *Basic Muffin*.

Makes 12 muffins

2 cups all-purpose flour
¼ cup sugar
   (for sweeter dessert muffins, use ½ cup sugar)
3½ teaspoons baking powder
1 egg
1 cup milk
¼ cup vegetable oil *or* melted shortening
½ teaspoon salt

1. Preheat oven to 400°F. (200°C).
2. Grease 12 large muffin cups.
3. Sift together flour, sugar and salt, and baking powder in a large bowl.
4. Beat together egg, milk and oil in a medium mixing bowl for 1 minute.
5. Add liquid to dry ingredients and stir only until combined.
6. Pour into muffin tins and bake in preheated oven for 18 to 20 minutes, or until golden brown.

* Reprinted with permission
from the *Purity Cookbook*.

Muffin Variations*

Cheese Muffins

Prepare muffins following basic recipe on page 7, but add ¾ cup grated cheddar cheese to dry ingredients before adding liquid. Combine and bake as per basic muffins recipe.

Wheat Germ Muffins

Prepare muffins following basic muffin recipe, but reduce flour to 1½ cups, and reduce milk to ½ cup. Stir in with *liquid ingredients*, a mixture of ½ cup wheat germ and ¾ cup boiling water. Bake as directed in basic muffins recipe.

Chocolate Chip Muffins

Follow basic muffin recipe on page 7 for the sweeter desert muffins. Then fold 1 cup chocolate chips into batter. Bake as directed for basic muffins.

Peanut Butter Muffins

Follow basic muffin recipe. Spoon half the batter into greased muffin cups. Top with 1 teaspoon peanut butter over each half-filled muffin cup, then cover with remaining batter. Bake as directed in basic recipe.

Potato-Cheese Puffs

Follow basic muffin recipe, but reduce flour to 1¼ cups, and stir into dry ingredients ¾ cup instant potato flakes. Sprinkle muffin batter in pans with mixture of ½ cup grated cheddar cheese and ¼ cup instant potato flakes. Bake as directed in basic muffin recipe.

Bacon Muffins

Chop and fry 5 strips of side bacon. Allow to cool. Prepare basic muffin batter from page 7, but substitute bacon and drippings for vegetable oil or melted shortening.

Pumpkin Muffins

Prepare basic batter, but add 1 teaspoon cinnamon and ½ teaspoon nutmeg to dry ingredients, and add ⅔ cup canned pumpkin with milk. Bake as directed in basic muffin recipe.

PEANUT BUTTER

* Reprinted here with permission, from the *Purity Cookbook*, page 198

8

Plain Muffins*

These are simple fare, requiring no special ingredients and you may find them a welcome change from fancier recipes in this book. These muffins are very good warm, split in half and served with a pat of melting butter.

Makes 12 muffins

2 cups all-purpose flour
3½ teaspoons baking powder
½ teaspoon salt
¼ cup sugar
1 cup milk
1 egg
¼ cup vegetable oil *or* melted shortening

1. Preheat oven to 400°F (200°C). Set shelf at centre level.
2. Grease 12 medium-sized muffin cups.
3. Sift or stir together flour, baking powder, salt and sugar in a large bowl.
4. In a medium bowl, beat together milk, egg and oil.
5. Stir liquid into dry ingredients, and only stir until combined. Batter should remain lumpy.
6. Fill cups 2/3 full.
7. Bake for 18 to 20 minutes or until golden brown.

* A *Purity Cookbook* recipe,
reprinted here with permission.

Variations to Plain Muffins

Cheese Muffins
Follow Plain muffins recipe except reduce shortening by 1 teaspoon, and add ½ cup grated cheddar cheese to dry ingredients.

Spice Muffins
Follow Plain muffin recipe, but increase sugar by 2 teaspoons and sift in 1 teaspoon cinnamon, ½ teaspoon nutmeg and ½ teaspoon allspice with the dry ingredients.

Blueberry Muffins
Follow Plain muffin recipe, and add 1 cup fresh blueberries *or* quick-frozen blueberries (*not* blueberry pie filling) to dry ingredients. Flour berries thoroughly by tossing them through dry mix. Then add liquid ingredients.

Orange Marmalade Muffins
Follow Plain muffin recipe but omit the sugar altogether. When adding milk to egg and oil, also add 3 tablespoons of orange marmalade.

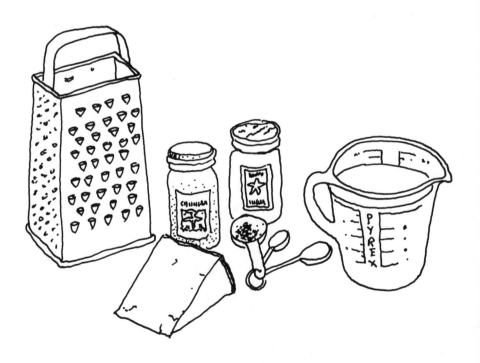

Basic Bran Muffins

An unadorned bran muffin recipe. Good hot with butter, or plain.

Makes 12 muffins

2 cups all-purpose flour
3 tablespoons sugar
3 teaspoons baking powder
½ teaspoon salt
1 egg
⅜ cup melted butter *or* salad oil
1⅛ cups milk
½ cup rolled oats
¼ cup 100 percent bran cereal (not bran flakes)

1. Preheat oven to 425°F (220°C).
2. Grease 12-cup muffin pan or use paper liners.
3. Sift flour with sugar, baking powder and salt in a bowl.
4. Beat egg with either butter or oil for 2 minutes, then stir into milk.
5. Stir oats and bran into flour, then make a well in mixed dry ingredients.
6. Pour into well, all at once, egg-oil-milk mixture.
7. Scraping bottom of bowl and stirring from the centre outward, make 12 to 15 circular strokes. The batter should remain lumpy.
8. Fill muffin cups almost to top.
9. Bake in preheated oven for about 25 minutes, or until well-browned.

Bran Muffins

Here is another of those classic rich bran muffin recipes.

Makes 30 muffins

1 cup cooking bran (such as Quaker Natural Wheat)
1 cup boiling water
1¼ cups sugar
¾ cup vegetable oil
2 eggs
2 cups buttermilk
2½ cups all-purpose flour
4 teaspoons baking soda
1 teaspoon salt
2 cups raisins *or* dates
2 cups bran buds (cereal)

1. Cover bran with boiling water, in a large bowl and allow to sit for about 1 minute or until mushy.
2. Add ingredients by stirring into the bran, in the same order as listed above.
3. Put batter in refrigerator to rest at least ½ hour before baking.
4. Grease 30 medium-sized muffin cups.
5. Preheat oven to 350°F (180°C) and when oven is hot, spoon batter into cups.
6. Bake on centre shelf for 20 minutes.

Note: Batter may be stored in refrigerator in a tightly covered container for up to 6 weeks.

Honey Bran Muffins

Try using buckwheat honey in this recipe for a really strong-flavored muffin!

Makes 12 large muffins

1¼ cups milk
1½ cups bran cereal
1 egg
⅓ cup vegetable oil
½ cup honey
1¼ cups all-purpose flour
1 tablespoon baking powder
½ teaspoon salt

1. Preheat oven to 400°F (200°C).
2. Grease 12 large muffin cups.
3. In a large bowl, combine milk with bran cereal.
4. Allow mixture to stand until milk is absorbed.
5. Add to bran/milk mixture, egg, oil and honey.
6. Beat mixture well for 1 minute.
7. Using another bowl, combine flour, baking powder and salt.
8. Add dry mixture to bran/liquid mixture.
9. Stir 12 to 15 times to combine dry and liquid ingredients. Batter should still be lumpy.
10. Pour or spoon into 12 well-greased muffin cups.
11. Bake on centre shelf for 25 minutes, or until brown.

These muffins are best served warm with a little butter on top.

Honey-Oat Bran Muffins*

Nutritious and tasty muffins. A good way to add fibre to your diet.

Makes 18 muffins

½ cup natural bran
1 cup rolled oats
¾ cup wheat germ
1 teaspoon cinnamon
½ teaspoon salt
1 cup sour milk*
¾ cup liquid honey
2 eggs, beaten
½ cup vegetable oil
1 cup all-purpose flour
2 teaspoons baking powder
1 teaspoon baking soda
½ cup raisins

*Note: Sour ordinary milk by placing 1 teaspoon vinegar *or* lemon juice in a measuring cup, *then* adding milk to measure 1 cup.

1. Preheat oven to 375°F (190°C).
2. Grease 18 large muffin cups.
3. Combine bran, oats, wheat germ, cinnamon and salt.
4. Add milk to above mixture, and let stand for ½ hour.
5. Now add the honey, beaten eggs and oil. Mix well.
6. Stir together flour, baking powder and baking soda.
7. Add to egg mixture all at once.
8. Stir just until moistened.
9. Add raisins to mixture and stir, a few times only.
10. Fill greased muffin cups 2/3 full.
11. Bake in preheated oven, on centre shelf, for 20 to 25 minutes.

* Reprinted with permission from *Canadian Living* Summertime Cookbook special, Aug. 1982

Anytime Bran Muffins

This recipe makes about 85 muffins!

If you are throwing a muffin party, or want to make muffins in commercial quantities, this recipe may be for you. It is also suitable for mixing in bulk and then storing in an airtight container for several weeks. You will need a *LARGE* bowl.

Of course, if you plan to use it all at once, you will require about 7 large muffin pans and a commercial oven, or the help of all your neighbours on both sides.

This batter is not stirred in the manner of most other recipes found in this cookbook.

5 to 6 cups whole-wheat flour
 (the larger amount *if* you find batter to be wet)
5 teaspoons baking soda
1 teaspoon salt (optional)
2 cups boiling water
2 cups cereal flakes (your choice — bran, corn, rice, oats)
1 cup butter
1 cup honey
4 eggs, beaten
1 quart buttermilk
4 cups unprocessed bran
½ cup raisins *or* chopped dates *or* currants
½ cup nuts (any kind *but* peanuts), finely chopped

1. Preheat oven to 425°F (220°C).
2. Grease the number of muffin cups you plan to use immediately, or line them with paper cupcake liners.
3. Combine flour, baking soda and salt, in a *very* large bowl.
4. Pour 2 cups boiling water over cereal flakes. Let cereal soak up water while you proceed with the next step.
5. In a large bowl, cream butter and honey. Beat eggs in a bowl.
6. In that bowl, combine 4 beaten eggs, buttermilk and blend this mixture with honey/butter mixture.
7. Add flour/soda mixture and blend gently by hand until well-mixed.
8. *Fold in* bran, soaked cereal flakes, raisins and chopped nuts. Do not stir this batter.

15

9. Spoon batter into prepared muffin cups, allowing about ⅓ of the cups for rising space.

10. Store any unused batter in an airtight container in the refrigerator or freezer. When next using it, spoon it out directly into the muffin cups *without stirring first.*

11. Bake muffins in preheated oven for 15 to 20 minutes. If not using all muffin cups in the pan, pour water to fill ⅔ of each empty cup to allow for even baking and to keep oven moist during baking. This also prevents damage to muffin pans, which may warp.

Note: Salt is optional in this recipe and makes little difference in the taste, given the large quantities of flour and bran.

Three Week Bran Muffins

These do not take 3 weeks to make. But the batter can be stored for up to 3 weeks so you can have a supply on hand for your short notice requirements.

> 1 cup boiling water
> 1 cup bran *(cooking type)*
> ½ cup shortening
> 1 cup granulated sugar
> 2 eggs
> 2½ cups buttermilk
> 2½ cups all-purpose flour
> 1 teaspoon salt
> 5 teaspoons baking soda
> 2 cups bran flakes *cereal*
> 1 cup raisins

1. This recipe does not begin with the usual preheating of the oven, as it is for those who wish to make up a batter and keep it ready for use on short notice.
2. Pour boiling water over bran and allow it to stand. Use *cooking* bran here!
3. While bran mix is cooling, cream together in a large mixing bowl, shortening, sugar and eggs.
4. Stir in buttermilk into creamed mixture.
5. Add bran-water mixture and stir in.
6. In another bowl, sift together flour, salt and soda, and add mixture to bran. Stir.
7. Add bran flakes *cereal* and raisins to mixture and stir again.
8. The mixture will be set aside for future use. Store it in an airtight plastic container with a snap-on lid, and keep it in the refrigerator.
9. Refrigerate at least 24 hours before using batter for baking.
10. When you wish to make a batch of muffins, do not stir batter. Scoop out batter, directly from container as it was stored.

11. Grease a medium muffin pan and preheat the oven to 375°F (190°C).
12. Fill muffin cups ⅔ full and place on centre shelf. Bake for 20 to 25 minutes.

Note: Variations of this recipe found in other sources say that the bat- can be kept in airtight containers in the fridge for 4 to 6 weeks. Try it if you wish, but the batter may become mouldy with long storage.

Note that this recipe used two different forms of bran.

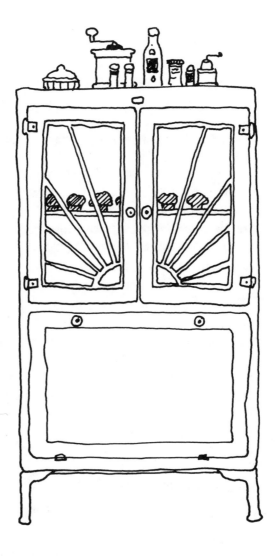

Six Dozen – Five Week
Refrigerator/Freezer Muffins

This recipe makes a batter specifically tested for its suitability for freezing, thawing and use on demand.

Makes 72 muffins

2 cups boiling water
2 cups 100 percent bran
3 tablespoons baking soda
3 cups sugar
1 pound shortening
4 eggs
1 quart buttermilk
5 cups all-purpose flour
1 tablespoon salt
4 cups bran flakes cereal
2 cups chopped raisins *or* chopped dates

1. Pour boiling water over mixture of 100 percent bran and baking soda in a large bowl.
2. Allow mixture to stand. It will fizz for a while.
3. Cream sugar, shortening and eggs in another bowl.
4. Add buttermilk to creamed ingredients, and stir in slowly.
5. Sift together flour and salt.
6. Add this to creamed mix.
7. Add remaining ingredients, then stir in bran and water mixture.
8. Stir until mixture is just blended and moist. Do not overstir.
9. This batter can be split into several batches, if desired, and sealed in airtight plastic containers. It may be refrigerated *or* frozen.
10. To use batter, grease a medium muffin pan and preheat oven to 400°F (200°C).
11. Spoon into greased pan enough to fill each cup ⅔ full.
12. If using frozen batter, thaw before attempting to use it.

13. Before freezing the batter, fill a muffin pan with the correct quantity needed for that size pan, remove and place batter in container for freezing. This will ensure that you only thaw exact amount needed.

14. Bake in preheated oven for about 20 minutes. You may use paper baking cups in this recipe for easy removal of muffins, and for neater handling and storage before eating.

Recipe provided by Sue Doddington,
of Newtonville, Ontario

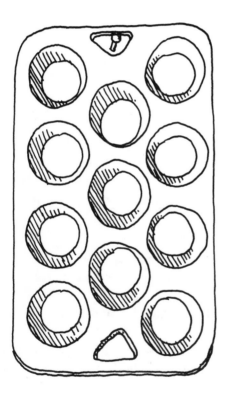
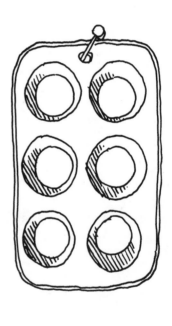

Old-Fashioned Muffins

Buckwheat Muffins

This grain imparts a strong flavor all its own to these muffins.

Makes 12 large muffins

2 tablespoons molasses *or* brown sugar
¾ teaspoon salt
½ cup cornmeal
2½ teaspoons baking powder
1 cup buckwheat (cereal or grain)
1¼ cups milk *or* 2½ cups buttermilk
2 egg yolks
4 tablespoons melted butter
2 egg whites, beaten

1. Preheat oven to 375°F (190°C).
2. Grease 12 large muffin cups.
3. Mix together sugar (or molasses), salt, cornmeal, baking powder and buckwheat.
4. In another bowl, mix together milk, 2 egg yolks and butter.
5. In another bowl, beat egg whites until stiff.
6. Add all liquid ingredients to the flour mixture, and stir a little.
7. Fold into mixture the 2 beaten egg whites. Stir just until moist.
8. Bake in greased pans on centre shelf for 20 minutes, or until golden.

Buttermilk-Cornmeal Muffins

A rich-tasting muffin with a warm golden color. If you can only obtain white cornmeal, these muffins will still have a pleasing (if pale) appearance, and you could always add a little yellow food colouring to the batter.

Makes 12 muffins

1½ cups yellow or white cornmeal
½ cup all-purpose flour
1 tablespoon sugar (optional)
4 teaspoons baking powder
1 teaspoon salt
¼ cup (½ stick) butter
¾ cup buttermilk
2 eggs

1. Preheat oven to 425°F (220°C).
2. Butter 12 medium muffin cups
3. Combine cornmeal, flour, sugar, baking powder and salt and mix thoroughly.
4. Melt butter over low heat. Let stand off heat for 2 minutes.
5. Stir into butter the eggs and buttermilk.
6. Stir butter mixture into dry ingredients and mix just until well-moistened but still lumpy.
7. Spoon batter into muffin cups.
8. Bake on centre shelf for 15 to 20 minutes, until lightly browned.
9. After removing muffin pan from oven, allow it to cool at least 5 minutes before removing muffins from the cups.

Cheddar-Cornmeal Muffins

Be sure to use home-grated cheddar cheese for the best possible flavor.

Makes 12 medium or 18 small muffins

1½ cups all-purpose white flour
½ cup cornmeal
1 tablespoon baking powder
½ teaspoon salt
pinch of cayenne red pepper
1 egg
1 cup milk
¼ cup (½ stick) melted butter
1¼ cups coarsely grated sharp cheddar cheese

1. Preheat oven to 425°F (220°C).
2. Butter a medium 12-cup muffin pan or 18 small cups.
3. In a large mixing bowl, combine flour, cornmeal, baking powder, salt and cayenne pepper.
4. In another bowl, beat egg with milk and melted butter.
5. Add liquid to dry ingredients and stir until thoroughly moistened.
6. Stir 1 cup of cheese into batter (reserving the rest).
7. Spoon batter into muffin cups.
8. Sprinkle about 1 teaspoon of remaining cheese over batter in each cup and place in oven.
9. Bake for 15 to 20 minutes or until golden in color.
10. Serve hot with butter on top (or freeze and reheat before serving).

The principal reason for failure of cornmeal muffins is using too little liquid. If the muffins come out too dry or too hard, try adding a little more liquid, either milk, honey, molasses or butter, next time.

Cheddar-Dill Muffins *

These don't taste quite like dill pickles, however, the dill does make them different!

Makes 12 muffins

2 cups of all-purpose flour
1 tablespoon baking powder
¾ teaspoon salt
2 tablespoons sugar
¼ cup finely chopped fresh dill
1 egg
1 cup plain yogurt
½ cup milk
3 tablespoons melted butter
½ cup grated sharp cheddar cheese
 (other cheese can be used instead of cheddar)

1. Preheat oven to 400°F (200°C).
2. Butter 12 medium-sized muffin cups.
3. Sift flour with baking powder, salt and sugar in a large bowl.
4. Stir in dill.
5. Combine egg, yogurt, milk and melted butter in a large bowl.
6. Gently stir liquid ingredient mixture into flour mixture until just combined.
7. Fold in grated cheddar cheese.
8. With an ice cream scoop, fill buttered muffin tins ¾ full.
9. Bake on centre shelf for 20 to 25 minutes or until done.
10. The muffins can also be brushed with beaten egg and sprinkled with sesame seeds, *before baking,* if desired.

*Reprinted with permission from *Canadian Living* magazine, Summertime Cookbook Special, August, 1982, p. 12

Cheese Muffins*

These muffins are best served hot from the oven, or rewarmed later, to bring out the rich flavor of the cheddar cheese.

Makes 12 muffins

2 cups all-purpose flour
½ teaspoon salt
¼ cup sugar
3½ teaspoons baking powder
¾ cup grated cheddar cheese
1 egg
1 cup milk
¼ cup vegetable oil *or* melted shortening

1. Preheat oven to 400°F (200°C).
2. Grease 12 medium muffin cups.
3. Sift together the flour, salt, sugar and baking powder. Stir in grated cheese.
4. Beat together egg, milk, and oil for 1 minute.
5. Stir liquid mixture into dry ingredients, *only* until combined. Batter should remain lumpy.
6. Fill prepared muffin cups ⅔ full.
7. Bake on centre shelf for 18 to 20 minutes, or until golden brown.

*from a Purity recipe, reprinted here with permission.

Cornmeal Muffins (1)

These are best hot from the oven, split and served with a pat of butter.

Makes 12 muffins

¼ cup butter, at room temperature
¼ cup sugar
1 egg, separated
1 cup all-purpose flour
¼ cup molasses *or* liquid honey
½ cup cornmeal
¾ cup cold milk
2½ teaspoons baking powder
⅓ teaspoon salt
¼ teaspoon baking soda

1. Preheat oven to 400°F (200°C).
2. Grease medium-sized 12 cup muffin pan.
3. Cream together butter and sugar.
4. Add egg yolk to the creamed butter and sugar, and mix in.
5. Alternately add a dry ingredient, stir, then a wet ingredient, stir in, then a dry ingredient, until all the ingredients except egg white are used.
6. Beat egg white, and fold it into the mixture. This makes muffins lighter. If you do not want to go to this trouble, then add the *whole egg* to creamed butter and sugar in step 4.
7. Spoon mixture into prepared muffin cups, filling 2/3 full.
8. Place pan on centre shelf of preheated oven, for 18 to 20 minutes or until done. (When this recipe is baked in a shallow cake tin, it is known as Johnny Cake.)

This recipe was provided by Helen Coburn of Cumberland, Ont. She says that you may use it as the basis of a cornmeal-bacon muffin by taking the following steps:
1. Omit molasses or honey
2. Take ¼ pound bacon, and fry until crisp.
3. Allow bacon to cool before adding to other ingredients.
4. Use only 1 tablespoon sugar.
All other ingredients are the same. When the bacon has cooled, add it, finely chopped, to the batter and stir in. You may save a small amount to sprinkle on top of each muffin before placing pan into the oven.

Cornmeal Muffins (2)*

A good basic muffin recipe. Delicious hot from the oven, split and buttered.

Makes 12 muffins

¾ cup cornmeal

1¼ cups milk

1 cup all-purpose flour

⅓ cup sugar

3 teaspoons baking powder

1 teaspoon salt

1 egg

¼ cup vegetable oil *or* melted shortening

1. Preheat oven to 400°F (200°C).
2. Grease 12-cup muffin pan.
3. Mix together in a large bowl, cornmeal and milk.
4. Allow mixture to stand for 5 minutes.
5. Sift together all-purpose flour, sugar, baking powder and salt in a medium bowl.
6. In a small bowl, beat egg with a fork.
7. Stir egg into cornmeal mixture, along with oil or melted shortening.
8. Add liquid mixture to mixed dry ingredients and stir until combined. Batter should be moist but lumpy. Do not overstir. Spoon into cups.
9. Bake in preheated oven 20 to 25 minutes, or until golden.

The principal reason for failure of cornmeal muffins is using too little liquid. If the muffins come out too dry or too hard, try adding a little more liquid, either milk, honey, molasses or butter, next time.

* A *Purity Cookbook* recipe, reprinted here with permission.

Cardamom Muffins

Cardamom seeds, crushed, or ground cardamom powder impart a special flavor to all baking.

Makes 24 muffins

1½ cups raisins
orange juice to cover raisins (exact quantity is variable)
2 tablespoons brandy
2 teaspoons grated orange rind
¼ teaspoon mace
¼ cup sunflower oil
½ cup honey
2 large eggs
¾ cup milk
1¾ cups all-purpose flour
¼ cup bran
½ cup wheat germ
⅛ teaspoon allspice
1 teaspoon cardamom
½ teaspoon salt
½ teaspoon baking soda
1½ teaspoon baking powder

1. Allow raisins to soak overnight, covered *first* with orange juice, *then*, with brandy, orange rind and mace added in quantity shown.
2. Preheat oven to 400°F (200°C), 12 hours after step 1.
3. Grease 24 medium muffin cups.
4. In a large bowl, mix together sunflower oil and honey.
5. Add eggs and milk to oil and honey mixture, and stir well.
6. In a medium bowl, combine flour and all other remaining ingredients.
7. Add flour mixture to liquid mixture, and stir a few times.
8. Drain raisins and discard orange juice/brandy liquid.
9. Fold drained raisins into batter and stir until all ingredients are moistened but lumpy. Do not overstir.
10. Spoon batter into prepared muffin pan and bake in preheated oven for 15 to 20 minutes.

Carrot-Wheat Muffins

The carrots add a moist but solid consistency to these muffins, and they do not turn them bright orange! A mildly spicy recipe for muffins.

Makes 12 muffins

1 cup whole wheat flour

1 cup all-purpose flour

1 teaspoon baking powder

½ teaspoon salt

¼ cup brown sugar

½ teaspoon cinnamon powder

⅛ teaspoon allspice *or* ground cloves

1 cup coarsely grated carrots

1 teaspoon orange rind, grated

1 cup milk

1 large egg

¼ cup molasses

¼ cup butter, melted

½ cup raisins

¼ cup nuts, chopped

1. Preheat oven to 400°F (200°C).
2. Grease 12 large muffin cups.
3. Using a large mixing bowl, measure and combine dry ingredients.
4. Stir the carrots and orange rind into the dry mixture.
5. In a small bowl, combine the milk, egg, molasses and melted butter, and beat.
6. All at once, add the liquid ingredients to the dry mixture.
7. Stir enough just to make the ingredients moist.
8. Now fold the raisins and nuts into the mixture.
9. Fill 12 large, greased muffin cups ¾ full with the batter.
10. On centre shelf of preheated oven, bake for 25 minutes.

This recipe originated with
the Ontario Milk Marketing Board.

Matzo Meal Muffins*

Makes 8 large or 16 small muffins

2 eggs
½ teaspoon salt
1 cup water
1½ cups matzo meal*
4 tablespoons rendered chicken fat

1. Preheat oven to 350°F (175°C).
2. Beat eggs with salt and water.
3. Stir in matzo meal to make a smooth batter.
4. Heat chicken fat and use it to lightly grease muffin pans.
5. Add any leftover fat to batter, stirring well.
6. Fill muffin cups ⅔ full. (Fill unused cups ⅔ full of water).
7. Bake on centre rack for 30 minutes, in preheated oven, or until brown.

*Note: This is a baked product, made from flour and water with no baking powder or yeast. It is baked as square sheets, then finely ground to the texture of cornmeal. It is sold in small boxes in food stores which sell Jewish food products.

* Reprinted with permission from the
Rochester Hadassah Cookbook;
Helen Hecker, editor.
Submitted by Inez Lipman.

Variations on Matzo Meal Muffins*

Variation 1
For sweet muffins use butter in place of chicken fat and milk in place of water. Grate a lemon rind. Add rind, 3 tablespoons sugar and 1 teaspoon cinnamon to the batter. Bake in the same manner as for Matzo Meal Muffins.

Variation 2
For a more delicate muffin, *omit* water and use matzo cake flour in place of matzo meal. It is also available at stores selling Jewish foods. Add ½ cup applesauce *or* ½ cup drained and chopped canned peaches to basic recipe. Add a dash of cinnamon *or* nutmeg for added flavor. Bake in buttered muffin pans, rather than pans greased with chicken fat. Serve with sliced, canned peaches or with a topping of applesauce.

Variation 3
Follow the same basic recipe for Matzo Meal Muffins. Add 1 cup soaked and pitted prunes, finely cut or chopped.

Variation 4
To basic recipe for Matzo Meal Muffins, add finely cut dates, raisins *or* chopped nuts. Or, you may mix in a mixture of all 3. Sprinkle tops of muffins with powdered sugar or top with any frosting of your choice.

* Reprinted with permission from the
Rochester Hadassah Cookbook;
Helen Hecker, editor.
Submitted by Inez Lipman.

Nutritious Muffins

These muffins are slightly crunchy with a nut-like flavor.

Makes 24 muffins

1 cup evaporated milk
¾ cup all-bran cereal
½ cup rolled oats
¾ cup whole-wheat flour
1 cup all-purpose flour
1 cup brown sugar
¼ cup wheat germ
1¾ teaspoon salt
1 teaspoon baking powder
½ teaspoon baking soda
½ cup shelled, unsalted sunflower seeds
2 eggs
½ cup vegetable oil
2 teaspoons vanilla extract
½ cup raisins
sesame seeds to sprinkle on top of batter

1. Preheat oven to 350°F (175°C) and grease 2 medium 12-cup pans.
2. Put milk, bran cereal and oats in a small bowl.
3. In a large bowl, mix remaining dry ingredients — whole wheat and white flour, sugar wheat germ, salt, baking powder, baking soda and sunflower seeds.
4. In a medium bowl, combine eggs, oil and vanilla with an electric mixer.
5. Add egg mixture to milk/cereal/oats mixture and stir.
6. Add wet-mixed ingredients to dry-mixed ingredients, stir in raisins.
7. Mix just enough to moisten all ingredients.
8. Spoon batter into muffin cups.
9. Sprinkle tops of muffins with sesame seeds for added nutty flavor.
10. Bake in preheated oven for 25 to 28 minutes, on centre shelf.

Thanks to Sue Doddington

Oat-Flour Muffins

You do not have to love oatmeal to enjoy these muffins.

Makes 12 muffins

2 tablespoons light brown (or golden yellow) sugar

2 cups oat flour (commercial flour, or oatmeal ground fine in a coffee-mill. If you grind it yourself, do just a little at a time, or you will clog the mill.)

3 teaspoons baking powder

1 teaspoon salt

½ teaspoon baking soda

1 egg

1 *or more* cups buttermilk

4 tablespoons melted butter

1. Preheat oven to 375°F (190°C).
2. Grease 12-muffin pan.
3. In a large bowl, stir together sugar, flour, baking powder, salt and baking soda.
4. In a small bowl, beat egg for 1 minute.
5. Add to egg ½ cup of buttermilk, and mix. Then add the melted butter.
6. Add the buttermilk/egg mixture to dry ingredients and stir until roughly blended.
7. Add more of the buttermilk, and stir as little as possible, trying to make a fairly smooth batter similar in texture to a cake mix batter. Keep adding buttermilk, stirring as little as possible, until you achieve the cake batter texture. Add no more buttermilk.
8. Spoon into greased muffin cups and bake for 15 to 18 minutes.

Oatmeal Date Muffins

A rather heavy, firm muffin. If you can't buy oat flour, you can make it yourself.

Makes 9 to 12 muffins

1½ cups oat flour (commercial oat flour
    or oatmeal ground fine in a coffee mill)
2 tablespoons brown sugar
½ teaspoon baking soda
2 teaspoons baking powder
10 to 12 dates, sliced or chopped
3 tablespoons melted butter *or* ¼ cup vegetable oil
2 egg yolks, well beaten
½ cup buttermilk (may require slightly more or less)
2 egg whites, stiffly beaten
½ teaspoon salt

1. Preheat oven to 375°F (190°C).
2. Grease 9 large or 12 small muffin cups.
3. Mix together in a large bowl, flour, sugar, baking soda and baking powder.
4. Stir in dates and flour them thoroughly.
5. In another bowl, mix butter or oil with beaten *egg yolks.*
6. Mix buttermilk and beaten egg yolk/butter mixture.
7. Add butter/yolks to flour mixture.
8. Fold in stiffly beaten egg whites. Stir until moist but lumpy.
9. Bake in prepared muffin pan in preheated oven for 18 to 20 minutes if using small cups, and 22 to 25 minutes if using large cups.

Note: If large cups are used, fill some of them ⅔ full with batter, and fill the others ⅔ full with water. Be careful when removing tins from the oven, that hot water does not spill on your hands!

Poppy-Seed Muffins

Another recipe with the poppy-seed lover in mind, with the added nutrition of whole wheat and wheat germ.

Makes 12 muffins

1½ cups whole wheat flour
½ cup wheat germ
2 teaspoons baking powder
½ teaspoon baking soda
2 beaten eggs
½ cup honey
1 cup commercial sour cream *or* yogurt
2 tablespoons cooking oil
½ cup poppy seeds

1. Preheat oven to 350°F (175°C).
2. Grease 12 large muffin cups.
3. In a large bowl, combine flour, wheat germ, baking powder and baking soda.
4. In another bowl, mix together 2 beaten eggs, honey, sour cream (or yogurt), and oil.
5. Add dry mixture to liquid ingredients and stir lightly 10 to 15 times.
6. Fold in ½ cup poppy seeds.
7. Spoon batter into prepared muffin cups.
8. Bake on centre shelf 25 to 30 minutes.

Rye and Rice Flour Muffins

A rich-tasting muffin, and very colorful if you use red currants.

Makes 9 large or 12 small muffins

½ cup brown rice flour

1 cup rye flour (light *or* dark)

¼ cup red *or* black currants

2 tablespoons brown sugar

1 teaspoon salt

1½ teaspoons baking powder

½ cup commercial sour cream

1 egg

¾ cup buttermilk

Note: Buttermilk may be replaced by ordinary milk.

1. Preheat oven to 375°F (190°C).
2. Grease 9 large or 12 small muffin cups and sprinkle a little white flour into bottom of each.
3. In a large bowl, mix together flours, brown sugar, salt and baking powder.
4. Stir in or toss currants through dry mixture to thoroughly flour them, which prevents them from sinking to bottom of batter during baking.
5. Beat egg in a medium-sized bowl.
6. Mix sour cream in with beaten egg.
7. Add milk gradually to sour cream/egg mixture and stir well.
8. Combine liquid mix with dry ingredients. After stirring in ½ cup milk, you may find batter is too dry. Add some more and stir in, until the batter is fluffy but still lumpy. Do not use all milk called for in recipe unless the batter requires it.
9. Spoon lumpy batter into greased and floured pan.
10. Bake in preheated oven, on centre rack for 15 minutes at 375°F (190°C) then turn oven down to 325°F (165°C) and bake for 5 more minutes. These muffins are best served hot with butter.

Sour Cream and Poppy-Seed Muffins

A rich and crunchy muffin.

Makes 12 to 15 muffins

2 tablespoons butter *or* ¼ cup vegetable oil
¾ cup sugar
2 eggs
½ cup poppy seeds (toasted *or* untoasted)
1 cup commercial sour cream
¼ cup milk
2 cups all-purpose flour
½ teaspoon baking soda
½ teaspoon salt
2 teaspoons baking powder

1. Preheat oven to 425°F (220°C).
2. Grease 12 muffin tins (large) or 15 muffin tins (small).
3. Cream together butter and sugar (or combine oil and sugar).
4. Add 2 eggs, and cream them into mixture.
5. Stir poppy seeds, sour cream and milk into mixture.
6. Sift together, in another bowl, flour, baking soda, salt and baking powder.
7. Stir dry mixture into liquid ingredients until mixture becomes moist but remains lumpy. The mixture will be quite thick and is supposed to be heavy! Stir only about 15 to 20 times.
8. Spoon into greased muffin pans and place on centre shelf in preheated oven for 20 minutes. Fill any unused muffin cups ⅔ full with water.

Sour Cream Muffins

It's recommended that those who are trying to put on some extra weight eat a few trays of these muffins.

Makes 12 to 15 muffins

½ cup light brown sugar

½ cup butter

2 eggs

2 cups all-purpose flour

3 teaspoons baking powder

½ teaspoon baking soda

½ teaspoon salt

1¼ cups commercial sour cream

Note: If you wish to replace all of the sour cream, use 1½ cups of butter-milk instead.

1. Preheat oven to 375°F (190°C).
2. Grease 12 to 15 muffin cups, depending on size of cups available.
3. Cream together sugar and butter until light and fluffy.
4. Beat eggs for 2 minutes.
5. Sift together dry ingredients in a large bowl.
6. Add beaten egg, sour cream, creamed butter/sugar mixture to dry mix.
7. Stir mixture 12 to 15 times.
8. Spoon mixture into muffin tins and bake on centre shelf for 20 to 25 minutes. Fill any unused muffin cups ⅔ full with water.

Sunflower Seed Meal and Oat-Flour Muffins

Makes muffins with a nutty flavor and a crunchy texture.

Makes 9 muffins

1 large egg

3 tablespoons melted butter

3 tablespoons brown sugar *or* honey

⅔ cup milk

1 cup oat flour (commercial oat flour or oatmeal ground fine in a coffee-mill)

¾ cup sunflower seed meal (made by *coarsely* grinding shelled sunflower seeds in a coffee-mill).

3 teaspoons baking powder

¾ teaspoon salt

1. Preheat oven to 375°F (190°C).
2. Grease and lightly dust with flour 9 large muffin cups of a 12-cup pan.
3. Beat egg in a small bowl.
4. In a medium bowl, mix egg, melted butter, sugar and milk.
5. In a large bowl, mix flour, sunflower seed meal, baking powder and salt.
6. Stir liquid mixture into dry ingredients, just enough to moisten.
7. Bake in prepared muffin cups in preheated oven for 15 to 18 minutes.

Note: Fill any unused cups ⅔ full with water. When removing pan from the oven, keep the pan level to prevent scalding yourself!

Sunflower – Sour Cream Muffins

Rich muffins with a nutty flavor. Very hard on low-calorie diets.

Makes 10 muffins

1 cup flour (rye, whole-wheat or oat)

¾ cup sunflower seed meal (this is available from health food stores or may be made by coarsely grinding shelled sunflower seeds in a coffee-mill)

2½ teaspoons baking powder

1 teaspoon salt

½ teaspoon baking soda

½ cup currants *or* raisins

2 tablespoons honey

¾ cup commercial sour cream

1 egg, well beaten

⅓ cup buttermilk

1. Preheat oven to 375°F (190°C).
2. Grease 12 large muffin cups.
3. In a large mixing bowl, stir together flour, sunflower seed meal, baking powder, salt and baking soda.
4. Stir into flour mixture the currants *or* raisins and thoroughly flour them to keep them from settling in the batter.
5. In another bowl, mix honey, sour cream and beaten egg. At this stage, *do not add the buttermilk* to the other liquids!
6. Combine liquid mixture with the dry ingredients in large bowl. Stir just until moist but lumpy — stir as little as possible.
7. Now begin adding buttermilk (not all at once!) and stir until batter starts to soften. How much you have to add will depend on the type of flour you have used. (Some absorb more liquid than others).
8. Spoon into muffin cups, filling 9 or 10 of them ¾ full. If you have a few empty muffin cups, partially fill them with water (½ full).
9. Bake in preheated oven for about 8 to 10 minutes.
10. Turn thermostat down to 325°F (160°C) and allow to continue baking at reduced heat for a further 8 to 10 minutes.

Sunflower — Whole-Wheat Muffins

This recipe yields the nutty flavor of sunflower seeds, without the crunch.

Makes 9 to 12 muffins

1 large egg, beaten

3 tablespoons melted butter

¾ cup milk

3 tablespoons brown sugar, lightly packed

3 teaspoons baking powder

¾ teaspoon salt

½ cup sunflower seed meal (available from heath food stores, or may be made from shelled sunflower seeds in a coffee-mill)

1¼ cups whole-wheat flour

1. Preheat oven to 375°F (190°C).
2. Grease 9 large or 12 medium muffin cups.
3. In a medium bowl, mix together the beaten egg, melted butter and milk.
4. In a large bowl, mix sugar, baking powder, salt, sunflower seed meal, and whole-wheat flour.
5. Stir liquid mixture into dry ingredients, only enough to moisten and make a lumpy batter.
6. Spoon batter into greased muffin cups, each ¾ full.
7. Bake in preheated oven for 12 to 15 minutes.

Best served hot with a pat of butter.

Sweet Jammies

These are something like the jelly doughnuts of the muffin family.

Makes 12 muffins

2 cups all-purpose flour
¼ cup sugar
1 tablespoon baking powder
½ teaspoon salt
¼ cup (½ stick) butter
1 cup unflavored yogurt
¼ cup milk
1 egg
½ teaspoon vanilla extract·
approximately ½ cup jam *or* fruit preserves
confectioners' sugar (optional)

1. Preheat oven to 425°F (220°C).
2. Grease cups of a regular 12-muffin pan.
3. Combine dry ingredients in a large mixing bowl.
4. Melt butter on low heat, then set aside for 2 minutes to cool.
5. Stir in yogurt and milk and mix well.
6. Beat egg and vanilla into liquid mixture.
7. Add butter mixture to dry ingredients and stir well.
8. Spoon half the batter into muffin cups.
9. Place about 1 teaspoon of jam over the batter.
10. Top jam with the remaining batter.
11. Place in preheated oven, and bake 15 to 20 minutes, or until golden brown.
12. Allow muffins to stand in pan for 5 minutes or more after you remove pan from the oven to prevent sticking.
13. (optional) Sift a little confectioners' sugar over top of muffins just before serving, if you prefer sweeter muffins.

Jam Surprise Muffins

The jam centre of these muffins takes all first-time eaters by surprise.

Makes 12 muffins

1¾ cups sifted all-purpose flour
¼ cup sifted soy flour
½ cup sugar
3 teaspoons baking powder
½ teaspoon salt
⅓ teaspoon grated nutmeg
1 egg
1 cup soy milk
¼ cup vegetable oil
¼ cup jam
  (your choice – apricot, peach, or other seedless jam)

1. Preheat oven to 400°F (200°C).
2. Grease 12 large muffin cups.
3. In a large mixing bowl, sift together white flour, sugar, baking powder, salt and nutmeg.
4. In a medium mixing bowl, beat egg with milk and oil for 1 minute.
5. Add liquid mixture all at once to dry ingredients and stir 12 to 15 times or until just moistened, but still lumpy.
6. Fill each muffin cup *just* ⅓ full, with a spoonful of batter.
7. With a clean spoon, place 1 teaspoon of jam over batter in each cup.
8. Spoon remaining batter into each cup, filling to within ⅓ of top.
9. Bake in preheated oven for 15 to 20 minutes.

Note: Soy flour is used in this recipe to aid in browning and to provide extra moisture in muffins (and other baked foods). You can also use soy flour to replace up to about 2 tablespoons *per cup* of all-purpose flour. Do not overdo it as the results can be unpredictable! As soy flour is moist (more moist than all-purpose flour), it packs a little tighter into the measuring cup. It should always be pre-sifted, therefore, and *then* measured out for quantity required in recipe. Soy milk is available in either a liquid *or* powdered form. Some stores sell a defatted soy milk, but this has less flavor and color than the full-fat product.

Whole-Wheat Muffins

High fibre, flavorful muffins.

Makes 12 muffins

2 eggs
⅔ cup warm milk
⅓ cup plain yogurt (commercial or homemade)
⅓ cup honey
2 cups whole-wheat flour
⅓ cup vegetable oil
½ teaspoon salt
1 teaspoon baking soda
¼ cup raisins (optional)
¼ cup chopped nuts, any type (optional)

1. Preheat oven to 425°F (220°C). Grease 12 large muffin cups.
2. Beat 2 eggs for 1 minute with electric mixer.
3. Add warm milk and yogurt and beat throughly with a wooden spoon.
4. Add honey and oil to mixture and stir in.
5. Add dry ingredients to liquid mixture and mix together thoroughly.
6. Pour batter into well-greased pans, about ⅔ full if batter did not include nuts and raisins, or ¾ full if you add nuts and raisins.
7. Bake for 15 minutes, or until done.

English Muffins

English Muffins

English Muffins bear no resemblance to the 95 percent of other muffins described in this book.

They are flat, 4 to 5 inches in diameter, and usually coated top and bottom with cornmeal. The leavening or rising agent may be either fresh yeast or what is known among bread bakers as "sourdough starter." Several recipes call for the dough (not batter), which has the consistency of bread dough, to be kneaded for a short time. One recipe calls for the use of a cookie cutter or wide drinking glass to cut the dough into round units for baking. Special English Muffin baking rings, made of sheet metal for the purpose, are available in some kitchen utensil stores. An equally practical substitute for manufactured baking rings can be made by taking discarded salmon or tuna fish cans, removing labels and cutting off lid and base with a can opener. Thoroughly clean interior of tin with hot soapy water so no fishy taste or smell remains to taint your muffins! Be careful that lid and base make a *clean break* away from tin. If a jagged edge is left at break-off point, it will cut your fingers when you remove the muffins. A sharp edge can be smoothed off with a metal file. (Not your good nail file, please!)

If you like English Muffins with a tangy flavor, I would recommend using the sourdough starter recipes. Making sourdough starter, which is contained in a recipe of its own, may take some practice and experimentation. It does not always work the first time. Don't be discouraged. Try again.

If you do not want to go to the bother of making and maintaining a supply of sourdough starter, recipes which call for use of packaged yeast will likely suit you better. To work well, yeast should be used within the "best before" date printed on the package, and should be kept cool and dry when not in use. A small amount should always be tested in a little warm water (in a prewarmed bowl) with 1 teaspoon of sugar added, to see that it is still active. If it is no longer active, and does not bubble and rise in the bowl within 5 to 7 minutes after testing, you need a new package of yeast. There are several varieties of packaged yeast — in "cake" form which is a solid lump that must be broken up to use it and a dry granular form. The package label gives specific instructions on how to activate yeast, which is a living micro-organism that gives off carbon dioxide bubbles (and alcohol) in the presence of sugar, moisture and warmth — 80°F to 100°F is the active range. Cooler temperatures will reduce bubbling to almost nothing. Higher temperatures will kill yeast. And killed yeast does not make dough rise. An accurate thermometer is advisable to ensure that optimum conditions for growth and gas production are maintained. Baking kills the yeast, but by then it has given off sufficient carbon dioxide bubbles to make dough light and cause it to rise. The other recipes in this book use baking powder or baking soda to chemically produce carbon dioxide gas, to make batter rise.

As yeast is a slow-acting leavening agent, English Muffin recipes need about 2 hours of your time, although 1½ hours of that is just to allow for rising.

English Muffins are generally "baked", actually fried, on top of the stove on a burner griddle, on an electric griddle or in an electric frying pan. One recipe calls for baking in an oven.

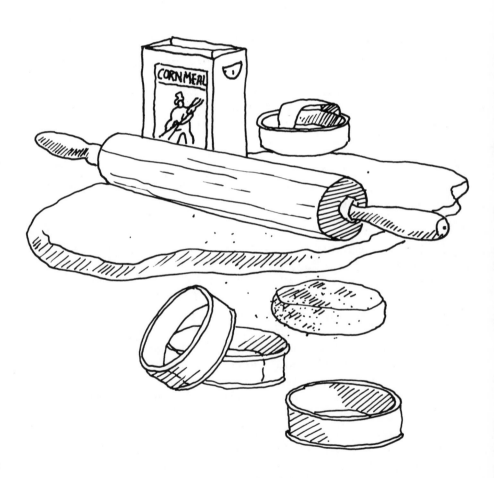

Whole-Grain English Muffins

Makes 15 to 18 muffins

1⅔ cups warm water

2 envelopes dry yeast
  (approx. 2 tablespoons compressed yeast)

¼ cup wheat germ

2 tablespoons honey

2 teaspoons salt
(optional, but muffins may not be very palatable without salt)

½ cup skim milk *powder*

½ cup rolled oats

1½ cups whole-wheat flour

2⅔ cups all-purpose flour

butter or margarine to grease bowl

¼ cup cornmeal

Utensils required:

  large mixing bowl — or 2, if you have 2

  measuring cup(s)

  electric beater

  wooden mixing spoon *or* large serving spoon

  tuna can cutter (see introduction) *or* muffin ring *or*
  wide-mouthed drinking glass

  baking sheet

  griddle (electric or stovetop) *or* electric frying pan

1. Preheat mixing bowl by letting hot water from tap stand
   in it for a few minutes. *Pour out this water,* as it is too hot for
   yeast.
2. Put 1-2/3 cups warm water (80° to 100°F *or* 25° to 40°C)
   into bowl, and sprinkle yeast over surface of water. A little
   white sugar may be added, but it is not necessary. Once
   yeast begins to foam, after about 5 minutes, proceed with
   recipe. If it does not foam, try again. If it *still* does not foam,
   you need a new supply of active yeast!
3. Once yeast is foamy, stir in wheat germ, honey, salt, powdered milk, rolled oats, all whole-wheat flour, *but only 1
   cup of white flour.* Set other flour aside for later use.
4. Using electric beater, beat batter for 5 minutes at medium
   speed.

5. Now add remaining 1¾ cups of flour to batter. Mix it in with wooden spoon.

6. Knead dough with your hands for 5 to 10 minutes. If you have not done this before, it will be tiring. But it must be thoroughly kneaded for at least 5 minutes to evenly distribute yeast and gas bubbles throughout dough.

7. If you have another large mixing bowl, grease right to top, and place dough in it to rest. If you only have 1 large bowl, then remove dough briefly, grease bowl and replace dough.

8. Cover dough with a sheet of waxed paper and a slightly dampened tea towel. Set dough aside for 1½ hours, until doubled in bulk.

9. Using knuckles of your closed fist, punch the dough down 2 or 3 times, to flatten it out in bowl.

10. Using your hands or a rolling pin, roll dough into a rectangular shape, about ½-inch thick, on a clean, flat surface.

11. Using a cookie cutter, English Muffin ring, tuna can cutter or wide-mouthed glass, cut dough into circles 3 to 5 inches in diameter.

12. Sprinkle cornmeal lightly over surface of baking sheet.

13. Place dough circles on baking sheet, spaced about 1 inch apart. If they touch, they will stick together.

14. Set aside for another 45 minutes in a warm place, to rise again and double in bulk. The dough should be covered for best results, with a lightly greased sheet of waxed paper, greased side against muffins.

15. After 45 minutes, carefully remove waxed paper and sprinkle any remaining cornmeal over muffins.

16. Heat griddle or electric frying pan to 275°F (130°C) and place a few muffins on heated surface. Fry each muffin for 6 minutes per side, then turn and fry other side for 6 minutes.

Potato-Whole-Wheat English Muffins

Mashed potato is used in these English muffins to make them a bit more solid in texture and to help hold them together. They are baked in the oven, rather than fried on a griddle.

Makes 12 muffins

1 small potato
1 package dry granular yeast
½ teaspoon honey
1¼ cups warm water
4 cups whole-wheat flour
1 cup cornmeal, to be used for dusting muffins

1. Boil the potato until completely tender, then mash with a fork.
2. Preheat oven to 375°F (190°C), if your kitchen is cool, so dough will rise.
3. In a large mixing bowl (which has been preheated) dissolve yeast and honey using ¼ cup of water. The remaining water will be used later.
4. Allow yeast mixture to stand until frothy, about 5 to 10 minutes.
5. Now pour remaining water into bowl, and stir in mashed potato and 3 cups of whole-wheat flour.
6. Turn dough onto lightly floured surface, and begin to knead. If dough is too sticky and pulls away from hands only with great difficulty, work in some more of remaining flour, a little at a time. If you do not require all the remaining flour, don't use it.
7. Knead dough until it becomes smooth and elastic in texture (8 to 10 minutes).
8. Using your hands or a rolling pin, spread dough out to about ½-inch thickness, in a rectangular shape.
9. With a wide-mouthed glass, large cookie cutter or a fish can ring (described in introduction), cut out about 1 dozen muffins.
10. Dust a baking sheet with cornmeal and spread muffins evenly over top.
11. Lightly sprinkle top of each muffin with cornmeal, and then place a dry dish towel or tea towel over top. Set baking sheet in a warm spot, either beside or a couple of feet above stove, or on top of refrigerator.
12. Allow muffins to rise for 1 to 1½ hours, or until double in bulk.
13. Bake in preheated oven at 375°F (190°C) for 6–8 minutes.

English Raisin Muffins

Those who like raisin bread will really enjoy these English muffins served hot, split and buttered!

Makes 10 to 12 muffins

1 cup warm water 80° to 100°F (25° to 40°C)
1 package dry granular yeast
1 teaspoon salt (optional)
3 cups all-purpose flour
¼ cup vegetable oil
2 tablespoons honey
½ cup brown raisins
¼ cup cornmeal

1. Warm a large mixing bowl by filling it with hot tap water, and let stand for 2 minutes. Discard water.
2. Pour in 1 cup warm water, and immediately add yeast.
3. Stir yeast until it dissolves, then let stand 5 to 10 minutes or until frothy.
4. Add next 5 ingredients. Stir until a smooth dough is formed.
5. Roll out dough on a lightly floured surface, using your hands or a rolling pin. It should be about ½-inch thick, and rectangular in shape.
6. Sprinkle half the cornmeal onto an ungreased cookie sheet or baking sheet.
7. With a round large cookie cutter (3½ to 4 inches in diameter), a wide-mouthed drinking glass or metal ring, (see English Muffin introduction), cut out 10 to 12 muffins and place on cookie sheet.
8. Sprinkle remaining cornmeal over top of each muffin and cover with a clean, lightweight tea towel. Set cookie sheet aside in a warm spot for one hour, or until muffins double in bulk. The top of the refrigerator is usually a good spot for this.
9. Preheat stove burner, when the muffins are almost fully risen. The burner should be about 375° to 400°F (190° to 200°C) or at a medium setting.
10. Place a griddle or cast-iron frying pan on the burner and put 3 or 4 muffins on to fry for about 7 minutes on *each* side. Adjust heat, if necessary, to prevent scorching of

muffins. Keep adding more muffins as you remove each group of 3 or 4, until all are fried.

Note: No grease is used on the heated surface.

11. These muffins may be served immediately, while hot, and are best when cut in half and served with butter spread on them. Or you can cool them and later split and toast them in your toaster, again served with butter! They're also delicious with a little honey or jam after you've buttered them.

Sourdough English Muffins

Sourdough English Muffins

Two recipes follow for Sourdough English Muffins.

If you already make sourdough bread, you can skip the instructions below for sourdough starter.

Sourdough gets its leavening or rising power from natural bacteria in milk products which have been allowed to sour in a controlled manner. Once you have made starter, which is the basis for sourdough breads and muffins, you can keep it in the refrigerator and replenish it as directed every couple of weeks (or store it in the freezer for several months). Each time you use some of the starter, you replace the amount used with equal amounts of warm milk and flour. This reactivates natural bacteria in the starter, and after a few hours the starter becomes bubbly again.

The bacteria which you want in your starter mixture comes from those present in yogurt, (either low-fat or plain unflavored commercial yogurt). By stirring in some yogurt, you "seed" the starter with desirable bacteria, which from then on, are always present. These bacteria give the sourdough recipe its characteristic sour and tangy flavor, and also make dough rise. In the first sourdough recipe, starter is used in dough without yeast, while in the second recipe, yeast is used in addition to starter.

Your attempts at making sourdough starter may not always work. If not, try again. Once you are successful, starter can be used and replenished for years. Use the same type of milk for each replenishing, and starter will not change flavor. Use either skim, low-fat or whole milk to begin your recipe. Each gives the recipe a characteristic taste. If you started with skim and later replenish with whole milk, the flavor of your sourdough starter and your muffins will be altered.

> To make your first batch of starter, you will need a 1-quart container. This can be stainless steel, glass or glazed pottery. *Rigid* plastic containers are also suitable.
>
> Begin by rinsing container under the hottest available water for several minutes. The fermentation will take place in this container.
>
> In a small pot or saucepan, heat 1 cup milk to 90° to 100°F (30° to 35°C) using a thermometer in the milk to be precise. Do not allow milk to get any hotter than this, or the desirable bacteria will be killed.
>
> Remove milk from heat and stir in 3 tablespoons of yogurt as specified above.
>
> Pour milk/yogurt mixture into warm container in which you

will store starter. Cover it tightly and set it aside to stand in a warm place, with a temperature of 80° to 100°F. (Some places to maintain this temperature: on top of your hot water heater, on top of your refrigerator or on a gas stove burner near *but not over* pilot light.)

You can also place starter in an electric oven, if you don't have any of the above places available. Carefully follow this procedure:

Move upper shelf of oven to a high level so that when starter container is placed on it, container will be 2" to 2½" below oven light bulb. The light bulb should not touch the top of the container, or the starter will get too hot and the bacteria will be killed.

Before placing the starter container in the oven to ferment, turn oven on to its lowest setting and allow the interior to become a bit warmer than room temperature. *Turn oven off.* Place starter container in the oven, directly in front of but not toughing oven light, and turn light on. Shut oven door, but leave it slightly ajar, perhaps held open with a wooden spoon.

The starter container must be allowed to stand undisturbed for 18 to 24 hours. Then open container and see what has taken place. If your starter is successful, it will have formed curds or lumps on top and have the same consistency as yogurt. If you tilt the container, the starter should be stiff enough to hold its position. If some clear liquid has risen to the top of the starter, stir it back in with a spoon.

If the starter liquid has changed to a light pink colour, however, the milk has spoiled rather than soured. The starter should be discarded, the container again rinsed with very hot water, and the procedure begun again.

Once you get the desired curd and yogurt-like consistency in your starter, proceed to the next stage:

Slowly stir into starter 1 cup all-purpose flour. Keep stirring until there are no lumps left from undissolved flour. Cover container tightly, and set mixture aside again in a warm place (80° to 100°F) to continue fermentation, this time for 3 to 5 days. Starter should be full of bubbles and take on a strong sour smell during this period.

When you check it, you may again note that some clear liquid has formed and risen to the top. If so, stir it back in. At this stage, it is also possible for the milk to break down and form a pink liquid. If this happens at the second stage, the mixture need *not* be entirely thrown away and begun again. (Don't be discouraged! A number of factors could account for the spoilage, such as excessive heat, overly cool storage conditions, presence of unfavorable bacteria in milk or yogurt, etc.). Remember that once you have a good batch of starter it can keep being replenished for months or sometimes years.

If it has started to go pink at this second stage, discard all but ¼ cup of starter and add in 1 cup of warm milk (90° to 100°F). Also blend in 1 cup flour. Cover container tightly and set aside in a warm place again for a few days until it is bubbling actively and has a strong sour smell.

The starter can now be used immediately or it can be kept in the refrigerator. You can also freeze it for 1½ to 2 months; more about this later...

If you use starter immediately in a sourdough recipe, you do not use the entire batch. Always leave about ½ cup of starter in the container, to seed the next batch. Then stir in equal amounts of warm milk and flour. For instance if a particular recipe calls for 1 cup of starter to be added to other ingredients, then replenish your container with 1 cup warm milk, and 1 cup all-purpose flour. If a recipe calls for ½ cup sourdough starter, then replenish container with ½ cup warm milk and ½ cup flour. *Milk and flour are mixed together first,* then added to starter container.

After replenishing (or "feeding" the starter) in this way, cover it tightly and let it sit in a warm spot for a few hours until bubbles again form in the mixture. The container can then be kept covered in refrigerator until the next time you bake. Allow starter to return to room temperature, *for about 4 to 6 hours* before you bake with it. Set container out the night before to warm up, if you prefer to bake in the morning.

If you use starter for frequent baking, it will stay active by replenishing with milk and flour as described above. If you do not bake regularly with starter, then to maintain its activity and sour taste, discard about ½ the starter from the container every 2 weeks, replenishing it with the proper mixture of new milk and flour.

If you choose to freeze starter, this should be done after it has been freshly "fed" with milk and flour mixture. This will commence activity. Then freeze starter, which slows fermentation, but allows it to continue for about 1½ to 2 months.

To use frozen starter, remove it from the freezer at least 24 hours before baking, and set in a warm place until it again becomes filled with bubbles.

If you bake bread regularly, you will note a certain feel to the dough. Sourdough has a slightly different feel after kneading than most doughs made to rise with yeast. When you touch it lightly with one finger, it may adhere or have a slightly sticky feel. Do *not* add more flour to reduce this slight tackiness (which you would do with regular bread dough).

Now that you have your starter, you are ready to make Sourdough English Muffins.

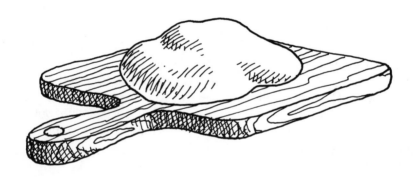

Cornmeal-Sourdough English Muffins

Delicious served hot straight from the oven, or allowed to cool, then cut in half and toasted in your toaster, served with butter! Depending on size of cutter used, makes about 12 muffins. *Make this recipe at night and allow to stand overnight before proceeding with final stages of baking.*

Makes 15 to 18 muffins

3⅔ cups whole-wheat flour

2 cups milk

1 cup sourdough starter (see instructions in previous section)

1 cup yellow cornmeal

1 teaspoon baking soda

3 tablespoons honey (liquid light honey *or* melted solid honey)

1 egg

1 teaspoon salt (optional)

1. In a large bowl, combine only 1½ cups flour, with milk, starter and cornmeal.
2. Cover bowl with waxed paper and a tea towel and let mixture rest overnight before proceeding.
3. Stir mixture down, as activity of starter will make it rise.
4. Add remaining flour, baking soda, honey, egg and salt. Mix well, then turn out dough onto a lightly floured surface for kneading.
5. Knead dough thoroughly for about 10 minutes, to work starter well through dough.
6. With your fingers or a rolling pin, roll out dough into a rectangular shape about ½ inch thick.
7. Cut into round muffin shapes with a wide-mouthed drinking glass, large cookie cutter (3½ or more inches) or metal English Muffin ring. Leave muffins on a lightly floured surface and cover with a tea towel.
8. Allow muffins to rise for 45 minutes, or until doubled in bulk.
9. Heat an electric frying pan or a griddle or cast-iron frying pan on top of the stove on medium heat, to about 300°F (150°C).

10. Fry 3 to 4 muffins at a time, for about 10 to 12 minutes per side. Do not fry each side more than one time! Serve immediately with butter on split muffins.

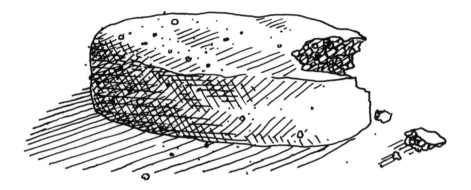

Yeast-Sourdough English Muffins

These muffins do not require the overnight standing period of the Cornmeal-Sourdough muffins. They combine rapid action of yeast in the rising process with the tangy flavor of sourdough. Well worth the effort in making them!

Makes 12 to 14 muffins

¼ cup yellow cornmeal (for dusting baking sheet)
½ cup sourdough starter
1 package dry granular yeast
¼ cup warm water (about 110°F) — use thermometer
1 tablespoon sugar
¾ teaspoon salt
1 cup warm milk (about 100°F) — use thermometer
3¾ cups all-purpose flour, unsifted

1. Dissolve yeast in warm water and "proof" it to be sure it is active, by letting it stand until frothy (5 to 10 minutes). Use large mixing bowl.
2. Stir into bowl the sourdough starter, milk, salt and sugar.
3. Stir in only about 3½ cups flour, enough to produce a stiff dough.
4. Turn out dough onto a lightly floured surface, then knead for 3 to 5 minutes, or until smooth.
5. If, during kneading, dough continues to feel sticky and is sticking to work surface, slowly add as much of remaining ¼ cup flour as is required to prevent further sticking.
6. Grease large mixing bowl and place dough in it.
7. Now turn dough upside down in bowl, so greasy side is up, and cover it with waxed paper and a light tea towel.
8. Set bowl aside to rise to double in bulk, for 1 to 1½ hours, in a warm location.
9. Once dough has risen to double, remove cover, and using your fist and knuckles, punch dough down flat.
10. Remove dough from bowl, onto a flat surface lightly dusted with part of the cornmeal.

11. Using your fingers or a rolling pin, pat down or roll out dough into a rectangular shape about ½ inch thick.

12. Cut dough into round muffin shapes about 3½ to 4 inches in diameter, with a large cookie cutter, English Muffin ring, wide-mouthed glass, or fish can ring. It helps to flour the cutter each time.

13. Place muffins on an ungreased baking sheet. (You may need two baking sheets). Sprinkle remaining cornmeal on top of muffins.

14. Again cover muffins and allow a second rise in a warm place. They should become puffy in about 45 minutes and are ready now for "baking".

15. Carefully uncover muffins and preheat cast-iron frying pan, stovetop griddle, or electric frying pan to about 275°F (130°C).

16. Frying surface should be lightly greased. Fry muffins for about 10 minutes on each side, until they take on a golden brown color.

17. Place muffins on wire cooling racks for 15 minutes, split open and toast. Serve with butter on split surface, and top with favorite jam.

Note: All sourdough muffin recipes leave you with some leftover dough after you have cut out your circles. You do not have to discard this dough. It can be rolled out to make 1 or 2 more muffins, allowed to rise for 20 minutes, sprinkled with cornmeal on both sides and fried. It may seem like trouble, but it is too good to throw away!

Fruit Muffins

Fruit Muffins

These muffins are naturally sweet, moist and flavorful.

Makes 18 small muffins

1 cup *fresh* fruit (black or red currants, cherries, blueberries, for example)

sugar to taste

⅓ cup butter

¼ cup light brown sugar

2 eggs, beaten

1 cup milk

2 cups sifted all-purpose flour

4 teaspoons baking powder

½ teaspoon salt

additional ½ cup fruit and light brown sugar

cinnamon and sugar mixture (5 parts sugar to 1 part cinnamon)

This recipe is not as straightforward as the others in the book. Read it through first, before going ahead with preparations.

1. Prepare a full cup of fruit sprinkled with sugar to taste, just before you are ready to add it to other ingredients. Grease 18 small or 9 large muffin cups.
2. Cream together butter and ¼ cup light brown sugar until smooth.
3. Beat 2 eggs for about 1 minute. Preheat oven to 375°F (190°C).
4. Add beaten eggs, milk and sifted dry ingredients to sugar/butter mixture. Stir in the one cup of fruit/sugar mixture. Mix about 10-15 times.
5. Half-fill muffin cups with batter.
6. Take **some** of the additional fruit-and-sugar mixture and add over batter in each cup, leaving space for a little more batter on top.
7. Now cover fruit in each cup with remaining batter, so cups are each about ¾ full.
8. Sprinkle top layer of batter in each cup with a mixture of cinnamon and sugar.
9. Bake in preheated oven at 375°F for 25 minutes.

Oatmeal Fruit Muffins*

Makes 12 muffins

1 cup all-purpose flour
3½ teaspoons baking powder
½ teaspoon salt
½ teaspoon cinnamon
pinch of nutmeg
¾ cup rolled oats
½ cup lightly packed brown sugar
¾ cup raisins *or* finely chopped dried apples
1 egg
1 cup milk
¼ cup vegetable oil *or* melted shortening

1. Preheat oven to 400°F (200°C).
2. Grease 12 medium-sized muffin cups.
3. Sift together flour, baking powder, salt and spices.
4. Stir in rolled oats, brown sugar and raisins.
5. Beat together, in another bowl, egg, milk and oil.
6. Stir liquid ingredients into dry ingredients, stirring only until combined. (Batter will be lumpy).
7. Fill prepared muffin cups ⅔ full.
8. Bake on centre shelf for 20 to 25 minutes.

(Apples and raisins may be left out and all other quantities remain the same, without substantially affecting the results).

* A Purity recipe, reprinted with permission.

Apple Crunch Muffins*

These muffins are made with a topping. The recipe is in two parts.

Makes 12 muffins

⅔ cup lightly packed brown sugar
⅓ cup all-purpose flour
2 tablespoons butter *or* margarine

Mix together the above ingredients until crumbly, and set aside to be used for topping after the batter is mixed.

1½ cups all-purpose flour
¼ cup sugar
3 teaspoons baking powder
½ teaspoon salt
½ teaspoon cinnamon
1 egg
¾ cup milk
3 tablespoons vegetable oil *or* melted shortening
½ cup applesauce

1. Preheat oven to 400°F (200°C). Grease 12 medium-sized muffin cups.
2. Sift together flour, sugar, baking powder, salt and cinnamon in large bowl.
3. In a medium bowl, beat together egg, milk and oil.
4. Add liquid ingredients to dry ingredients and stir only until combined to make a lumpy batter.
5. Fill muffin cups ⅔ full.
6. Spoon 1 teaspoon applesauce over top of batter in each cup.
7. Sprinkle reserved crumbly topping onto applesauce. Depending on how thick you make topping, some of the mixture may be left over.
8. Bake in preheated oven on centre shelf for 18 to 20 minutes, or until golden brown in color.

* A Purity recipe, reprinted with permission.

Applesauce Muffins

This is even better when made from homemade applesauce, with small chunks of apple in it.

Makes 16 muffins

2 cups sifted pastry flour
2 teaspoons baking powder
¾ teaspoon salt
1 teaspoon cinnamon
¼ teaspoon allspice
⅛ teaspoon ground cloves
¾ cup brown sugar
¾ cup raisins
¼ cup unblanched almonds
4 tablespoons shortening
1 egg
1 cup cold applesauce

1. Preheat oven to 400°F (200°C) and grease 16 large muffin cups.
2. Mix and sift flour, spices, and other dry ingredients in a large bowl.
3. Wash and pat dry (with a towel) raisins and nuts.
4. Using two knives cut shortening into dry ingredients until it resembles a coarse meal.
5. Chop the nuts.
6. After beating egg in a small bowl, add applesauce.
7. Combine liquid ingredients with dry ingredients.
8. Stir until dry ingredients are moistened but lumpy. Do not overstir.
9. Spoon batter into prepared muffin cups. Fill any unused cups with water to about ⅔ full.
10. Bake in preheated oven for about 20 minutes.

Applesauce Spice Muffins*

A moist, apple-flavoured muffin, with a hint of cinnamon.

Makes 12 muffins

1¼ cups cake and pastry flour
3 teaspoon baking powder
½ teaspoon salt
½ teaspoon cinnamon
¼ teaspoon nutmeg
¼ cup granulated sugar
1 cup whole bran cereal
1 egg
⅓ cup milk
¼ cup vegetable oil *or* melted shortening
⅔ cup thick unsweetened applesauce

1. Preheat oven to 400°F (200°C).
2. Grease 12 medium-sized muffin cups.
3. Sift or blend together flour, baking powder, salt, spices and sugar.
4. Stir in bran cereal.
5. In another bowl, beat together egg, milk, oil, and applesauce.
6. Stir liquid ingredients into dry mixture, and stir only until combined. Batter will remain lumpy.
7. Fill greased muffin cups ⅔ full.
8. Bake in preheated oven, on centre shelf, for 20 to 25 minutes.

* A Purity recipe, reprinted
with permission.

Diet (low-calorie) Apple Muffins *

If you love tasty muffins but have to be cautious about calories, this recipe is ideal.

Makes 6 muffins

3 apples
3 eggs
3 tablespoons powdered sugar substitute (Do not use Aspartame®)
½ teaspoon vanilla extract
¼ teaspoon powdered cinnamon
¼ teaspoon powdered nutmeg
½ teaspoon orange extract
3 slices bread

1. Preheat oven to 375°F (190°C).
2. Grease 6-cup muffin pan.
3. Peel and core apples.
4. Grate apples and set aside.
5. Beat eggs.
6. Add spices (cinnamon, vanilla, orange, nutmeg) to beaten eggs. Stir in sugar substitute.
7. Break bread into small pieces and add to mixture.
8. Stir in apples, mixing all together well.
9. Spoon batter into greased muffin cups.
10. Bake in preheated oven for 45 minutes on centre rack.

* Reprinted with permission from the
Rochester Hadassah Cookbook;
Helen Hecker, editor. Submitted by
Gloria Brauer.

74

Banana Muffins

A tasty way to make use of the ripe bananas you may otherwise not eat.

Makes 12 muffins

½ cup butter *or* shortening
1 cup sugar
1 egg
1 cup ripe bananas (medium to large size)
1 teaspoon baking soda
1½ cups all-purpose flour
½ teaspoon salt
2 tablespoons hot water

1. Preheat oven to 375°F (190°C). Place shelf on centre level of oven.
2. Grease 12 medium muffin cups.
3. Cream together butter and sugar in a large bowl.
4. Peel ripe bananas, and using a fork, mash until no lumps remain.
5. Blend egg into creamed sugar/butter mixture and then mix into it the mashed bananas.
6. In hot water, dissolve baking soda. Add it to sugar/bananas.
7. Combine sugar/banana mixture with flour and salt and stir.
8. Keep stirring only until blended, about 15 to 20 times maximum. Mixture should be lumpy.
9. Spoon batter into greased muffin pan and bake in preheated oven for 20 minutes, or until golden brown.

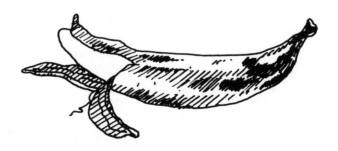

Banana Bran Muffins

These are wholesome, high-fibre muffins, with the banana lover in mind. If you want a stronger banana taste in your muffins, extra flavor can be added.

Makes 18 muffins

2 large or medium ripe bananas
1 tablespoon lemon juice
⅓ cup molasses
⅓ cup vegetable oil
2 eggs
½ teaspoon banana extract (optional)
1¼ cups sifted all-purpose flour
¾ cup natural flaked bran
2 tablespoons wheat germ
1 tablespoon baking powder
½ teaspoon salt (optional)
¼ teaspoon baking soda
½ cup chopped walnuts
½ cup raisins

1. Preheat oven to 400°F (200°C).
2. Grease 18 muffin cups.
3. Slice peeled bananas and place in food blender.
4. Add lemon juice to blender and puree until mixture is smooth. This should give you about 1 cup of liquid.
5. Spoon banana puree into large bowl.
6. Add molasses, vegetable oil, eggs (and extract, if used) and mix until well blended with banana puree.
7. In another bowl, combine dry ingredients with raisins.
8. To above mixture, add bananas all at once and stir until well mixed but still lumpy—don't overstir.
9. Fill 16 to 18 muffin cups with batter, each ⅔ full.
10. Bake in preheated oven on centre shelf for 20 to 25 minutes, or until lightly browned.

Banana-Wheat Germ Muffins

Nutritious, mildly spicy muffins with the banana lover in mind. They have a little crunchiness added in the form of walnuts.

Makes 12 muffins

2 eggs
1 cup mashed ripe banana (about 2 large bananas)
½ cup milk
¼ cup (½ stick) melted butter
1½ cups all-purpose flour
1 cup toasted wheat germ
1 tablespoon baking powder
1 teaspoon ground nutmeg
1 teaspoon salt
½ cup brown sugar
½ cup chopped walnuts

1. Preheat oven to 425°F (220°C).
2. Grease muffin cups of a regular 12-cup pan.
3. Beat together eggs, bananas, milk and butter in a medium bowl until smooth.
4. Combine flour, wheat germ, baking powder, nutmeg, salt and sugar.
5. Add liquid ingredients to dry mixture and stir until well-moistened.
6. Now mix in chopped walnuts.
7. Spoon batter into muffin cups to ¾ full.
8. Bake in preheated oven on centre rack for about 20 minutes, or until muffins take on a rich brown color.

Delicious with butter or a wedge of old cheddar cheese.

Wheat-Free Banana Cornmeal Muffins

A delicious muffin for those who must limit their intake of wheat products

Makes 12 muffins

2 teaspoons honey
¼ cup oil
1 egg, well beaten
1 teaspoon vanilla extract
1 cup mashed ripe banana
1 cup cornmeal
1 cup rolled oats (not instant oatmeal)
1 tablespoon baking powder
½ teaspoon cinnamon
¼ teaspoon allspice
1 cup any nuts except peanuts (optional)
½ cup raisins (optional)

1. Preheat oven to 350°F (175°C) and grease 12 large muffin cups. (If nuts and raisins are added, you may require several more muffin cups. Grease 4 to 6 more and have them ready.)
2. In a medium bowl, first mix honey, oil, beaten egg and vanilla.
3. Place mashed banana in a large bowl.
4. Add liquid mixture to mashed banana and stir lightly.
5. In a large bowl, combine cornmeal, oats, baking powder and spices. If you are using nuts and/or raisins, add them at this point and toss well to coat them thoroughly.
6. Add liquid mixture to dry ingredients and stir 10 to 15 times. Batter should remain lumpy.
7. Spoon into prepared muffin cups and bake for 20 minutes.

If muffins come out too dry for your taste, add ¼ cup water to step 4 next time.

Blueberry Muffins

Makes 12 muffins

1 cup all-purpose flour

1 cup whole-wheat flour

½ cup *plus* 1½ tablespoons sugar

1 tablespoon baking powder

½ teaspoon salt

½ teaspoon cinnamon powder

1½ to 2 cups fresh (or frozen unthawed) blueberries
— see note below

¼ cup butter, melted

½ cup milk

2 eggs

½ teaspoon vanilla extract

Note: If you use larger quantity of blueberries, you may experience difficulty in removing muffins from the pan. It is best to let muffins cool before trying to remove them, and reheat them at 350⁰F before serving. Reheat them at this temperature for 6 to 7 minutes.

1. Grease the muffin cups of a regular pan heavily with butter. Also grease top surface of pan. You may line with paper cups.
2. Preheat oven to 425°F (220°C).
3. In a large bowl, combine the following dry ingredients: all flour, ½ cup sugar, baking powder, salt and cinnamon.
4. In a separate bowl, toss together 1 tablespoon of dry mixture with blueberries. Set aside.
5. Melt butter, then allow to cool slightly.
6. Add milk to butter, stirring well.
7. To butter and milk mixture, stir in eggs and vanilla.
8. Add egg mixture to dry ingredients and stir until moistened thoroughly.
9. Stir in berries.
10. Spoon batter into well-buttered muffin cups.
11. Sprinkle muffin tops with reserved 1½ tablespoons sugar.

12. Bake in preheated oven on centre shelf for 15 minutes or until golden brown.
13. Wait at least 5 minutes before removing muffins from pan.

Diabetic Blueberry Muffins (Fresh Blueberries)

These delicious muffins are especially formulated for a no-sugar diet.

Makes 12 muffins

	Carbohydrates (gm)	Protein (gm)	Fat (gm)
2 cups Bisquick®	152	19	29
approx. ¼ cup artificial sweetener * (equivalent to 6 tablespoons sugar)			
1 cup commercial sour cream			40
1 egg		7	5
1 cup fresh blueberries	15		
2 teaspoons grated lemon peel			
	167	26	74
1 serving equals 119 calories	14	2	6

1. Preheat oven to 425°F (210°C) and grease 12-cup muffin pan.
2. Combine Bisquick® and ¼ cup artificial sweetener.
3. Make a well in centre of mixture and add sour cream and egg all at once.
4. Beat with a fork until ingredients are well combined.
5. Gently fold in fresh blueberries.
6. Put ¼ cup of batter into each muffin cup.
7. In a small bowl, combine lemon peel and 2 tablespoons artificial sweetener*.
8. Sprinkle, peel and sweetener mix over batter in each muffin cup.
9. Bake on centre shelf for 20 to 25 minutes, or until golden brown. These muffins are best served hot.

Exchange per serving: 1 bread, 1 fat

Note: This recipe was provided by dieticians of several hospitals. It appears to have come from the *Comprehensive Diabetic Cookbook*, by Dorothy Kaplan, published in 1972 by Frederic Fell, Inc.

* Do not use Aspartame® sweetener in this recipe or any baked recipe. Aspartame® breaks down chemically when subjected to heat, and its sweetening property is destroyed.

Wheat-Free, Rice-Flour Blueberry Muffins

This recipe will be welcomed by those who must exclude wheat from their diet.

Makes 12 muffins

2 cups rice flour
4 teaspoons baking powder
½ cup honey
3 tablespoons vegetable oil
2 beaten eggs
1 teaspoon vanilla extract
1¼ cups frozen or fresh blueberries
   (*not* blueberry pie filling)

1. Preheat oven to 350°F (175°C).
2. Grease 12 large muffin cups.
3. In a large bowl, combine rice flour and baking powder.
4. In another bowl, combine honey, oil, beaten eggs and vanilla.
5. Mix liquid ingredients into dry mixture.
6. Fold blueberries into batter.
7. Fill muffin cups ¾ full.
8. Bake on centre shelf of oven for 20 minutes.

Blueberry Oatmeal Muffins

A rather sweet muffin. Depending on the brand of commercial blue-berry yogurt you use, the finished product may have whole blueberr-ies or finely chopped ones.

Makes 12 muffins

1 egg
3 tablespoons butter
¼ cup light honey
½ cup milk
1 cup blueberry yogurt
1 cup uncooked rolled oats
1 cup whole-wheat flour
½ cup all-purpose flour
3 teaspoons baking powder
1 teaspoon baking soda
½ teaspoon salt
¼ cup sugar

1. Grease 12-cup muffin pan.
2. Preheat oven to 400°F (200°C).
3. Beat egg for 3 minutes
4. Melt butter in small pan.
5. Measure honey and stir in melted butter until well combined.
6. Add honey-butter mixture to beaten egg and stir in milk.
7. Add yogurt to honey, butter and egg mixture, and beat well for 1 minute.
8. Stir in oats until well moistened. Let sit 1 minute.
9. Sift together, in another bowl, whole-wheat flour, white flour, baking powder, baking soda, salt and sugar. Mix dry.
10. Add dry-mixed ingredients to liquid mixture in large bowl and stir 15 to 20 times maximum. Stir to moisten, but leave batter lumpy.
11. Spoon batter into muffin cups.
12. Place on centre shelf of preheated oven, and bake 20 to 25 minutes, or until brown.

Cherry Muffins

This recipe produces muffins with a pinkish tinge, and a luscious flavor of cherries.

Makes 12 muffins

1½ cups candied maraschino cherries
2 cups whole-wheat flour (sift before measuring, and add back any bran which is trapped in the sifter screen)
2½ teaspoons baking powder
1 teaspoon salt
1 egg
⅓ cup butter
⅓ cup brown sugar
1 tablespoon lemon juice
1 cup milk

1. Grease 12 large muffin cups.
2. Preheat oven to 425°F (220°C) and place rack on centre shelf.
3. Slice cherries in halves or quarters, on a cutting board.
4. Combine flour, baking powder and salt in a large bowl.
5. In a medium bowl, beat together egg and butter for about 1 minute.
6. Add sugar and lemon juice, and beat again for 1 minute.
7. Add milk and beat again for a minute. (Lemon juice may curdle milk or butter. This is normal and will not spoil batter.
8. Add cherry pieces to dry ingredients.
9. With a fork, stir cherries in to dry ingredients so they become thoroughly floured. (If cherries are sticky when added to flour, stir until they are fully separated from each other.)
10. Make a well in the centre of flour mixture.
11. Pour liquid into well.
12. Stir 15 to 20 times maximum, using a fork, and make full circles begining in centre and stir to outer edge of bowl. All ingredients should be moistened but batter must remain lumpy. Be sure that a little flour remains dry, however.

13. Immediately spoon batter into greased muffin cups, filling them ¾ full and place in preheated oven.
14. Bake for 20 minutes on centre shelf.

Cranberry Orange Muffins

An excellent use for leftover cranberry sauce, and a very simple recipe, too!

Makes 30 medium or 18 large muffins

3 cups whole-wheat flour
½ cup honey
½ cup chopped nuts (any kind except peanuts)
2 teaspoons baking powder
1 teaspoon salt (optional)
1 teaspoon baking soda
¼ cup freshly squeezed orange juice
3 teaspoons vegetable oil *or* melted shortening
1 egg
2 cups whole cranberry sauce (homemade or frozen)
½ cup water (optional, if your cranberries seem quite dry)

1. Preheat oven to 400°F (200°C).
2. Grease 30 medium or 18 large muffin cups.
3. Combine all ingredients together in a large bowl.
4. Using a large spoon or rubber spatula, mix all ingredients well. Add extra water, if batter is too dry.
5. Fill greased muffin tins ⅔ full.
6. Bake in preheated oven on centre rack for 15 to 20 minutes.

Crunchy Oat and Cranberry Muffins

Makes 12 muffins

¾ cup all-purpose flour
¾ cup whole-wheat flour
1 cup oatmeal *(do not use quick or instant oatmeal)*
½ cup brown sugar
1 tablespoon baking powder
1 teaspoon salt
1 teaspoon cinnamon
1 cup fresh *or* frozen cranberries
¼ cup (½ stick) butter
1 cup milk
1 egg

1. Preheat oven to 425°F (220°C).
2. Butter cups of a regular 12-cup muffin pan.
3. Combine dry ingredients (except cranberries) in a large mixing bowl. Be sure they are well mixed.
4. In a separate bowl, toss cranberries with 1 tablespoon of dry mixture to flour them thoroughly, then set aside until later.
5. Melt butter over low heat, and remove from stove to cool for several minutes.
6. Stir milk into melted butter, then stir in the egg.
7. Stir butter mixture into dry ingredients in large bowl and mix well.
8. Stir in cranberries, and be sure they are well distributed. Don't overstir.
9. Spoon batter into greased muffin cups, and bake in a preheated oven for 15 to 20 minutes or until lightly browned.
10. Allow to stand and cool at least 5 minutes before removing from pan.

Date – Honey – Carrot Muffins

A heavier muffin, with a taste of honey. Carrots and dates give it firmness.

Makes 12 muffins

¼ cup (½ stick) butter
½ cup honey
½ cup milk
2 eggs
1 cup all-purpose flour
1 tablespoon finely grated orange peel
1 tablespoon baking powder
1 cup whole-wheat flour
1 teaspoon salt
1 cup grated carrots
1 cup diced, pitted dates

1. Preheat oven to 425°F (220°C).
2. Grease 12 medium-sized muffin cups.
3. Melt butter with the honey.
4. Take butter/honey mixture off heat and allow to cool for a few minutes.
5. Stir in the milk.
6. Stir in eggs and orange peel.
7. Beat to blend, then set mixture aside.
8. In a large bowl, combine dry ingredients, except carrots and dates.
9. Stir in butter mixture.
10. When butter mixture is incorporated, stir in carrots and dates.
11. Spoon batter into muffin pan to ⅔ full.
12. Bake 15 to 20 minutes in preheated oven, or until toothpick inserted into centre of muffin comes out clean.
13. Let stand for at least 5 minutes before attempting to remove from pan.
14. Serve warm with butter or cream cheese and orange marmalade.

Trinidad Curry Date Muffins[*]

If you enjoy curry dishes, these muffins are for you. Best hot from the oven, they smell delicious while baking.

Makes 12 muffins

1 tablespoon bran
2 cups all-purpose flour
1½ teaspoon mild *(not hot!)* curry powder
½ cup brown sugar, lightly packed
½ teaspoon salt
3½ teaspoons baking powder
¾ cup chopped pitted dates
1 egg
¼ cup vegetable oil *or* melted shortening
1¼ cups milk

1. Preheat oven to 400°F (200°C).
2. Grease 12 large muffin cups.
3. Combine bran, flour, curry powder, sugar, salt and baking powder in a large bowl.
4. Add dates, and stir to thoroughly flour date pieces.
5. In another bowl, mix egg, oil, milk and beat for 2 minutes.
6. Add liquid ingredients to dry mixture, and stir 15 to 20 times.
7. Spoon batter into prepared muffin pan and bake in preheated oven for 20 minutes.

Note: The curry flavor of these muffins is not long-lasting. You will find that it becomes less after a day and may be undetectable after that. Do not be tempted to use *hot* curry powder to make the flavor last, unless you like hot muffins the first day; otherwise they may not be edible, fresh from the oven or the rest of that day. If you find 1½ teaspoons too hot, reduce by ½ teaspoon.

[*] Suggested by Joyce Calvert,
a transplanted Trinidadian living in Cumberland, Ontario

Fig Orange Muffins

The fig seeds add crunch to this muffin.

Makes 12 muffins

Use basic muffin recipe on page 7 and stir in the following ingredients:

½ cup chopped dried figs
¾ teaspoon grated orange peel

You will also need a little orange marmalade for topping.

1. Preheat oven to 425°F (220°C) and grease 12 large muffin cups.
2. Prepare basic muffin recipe.
3. Mix figs and orange peel with dry ingredients.
4. Blend in liquid ingredients just until dry mixture is moist — there will still be lumps in the batter.
5. Bake in preheated oven for 20 to 25 minutes, or until well browned.
6. Serve hot, with a teaspoon of orange marmalade on top of each muffin.

Grapefruit Muffins with Nuts

Now these are different. The grapefruit flavor is quite tangy. This recipe was reworked from one which called for orange peel. That day, I had no oranges!

Makes 18 medium-sized muffins

1 cup whole-wheat flour
½ cup white sugar
3 teaspoons baking powder
1 teaspoon salt
¾ cup *mixed* finely chopped walnuts and peanuts
3 cups raisin bran cereal
⅓ cup bran
2 eggs (medium)
½ cup orange juice
1 cup milk
¼ cup cooking oil
⅓ cup finely grated peel of about ¼ grapefruit

1. Preheat oven to 400°F (200°C).
2. Grease 18 medium-sized muffin cups.
3. Combine flour, sugar, baking powder, salt and chopped nuts in a large bowl.
4. Crush raisin bran cereal and bran into fine crumbs and add to flour mixture, stirring them in uniformly.
5. Make a well in centre of dry ingredients.
6. Combine in a large bowl, the egg, grapefruit rind, orange juice, milk and oil.
7. Add liquid mixture to well in the dry mixture, and blend in with a fork, using 20 to 25 turns and working mixture out from centre to edges of bowl.
8. Fill muffin tins ¾ full and bake in preheated oven for 20 minutes.

Lemon Muffins

Different from the other lemon muffin recipe in this book; these get their flavor from fresh frozen lemonade.

Makes 12 to 15 muffins

½ cup (¼ pound) butter *or* margarine
3 large eggs
¼ cup sugar
1 teaspoon baking powder
1 cup all-purpose flour, sifted before measuring
½ cup undiluted frozen lemonade concentrate *(thawed)*
½ teaspoon salt

1. Preheat oven to 375°F (190°C).
2. Grease 12 medium-sized or 15 small muffin cups.
3. Cream together sugar and butter until they are of a creamy consistency.
4. Add eggs, then beat mixture until light.
5. Sift flour (again) with baking powder and salt.
6. Add flour mixture to creamed ingredients, *alternately* with some of the lemonade, until both are completely used. Stir between additions.
7. Fill prepared muffin cups each ⅔ full of batter.
8. Bake in preheated oven for 20 minutes, or until lightly browned.

Note: Medium-sized muffin tins are 2½ inches in diameter.
   Small cups are 2 inches in diameter.

Rich Lemon Muffins

Makes 12 muffins

½ cup *plus* 2 tablespoons sugar
1 tablespoon baking powder
1 teaspoon salt
2 cups all-purpose flour
½ cup (1 stick) butter
¾ cup fresh lemon juice
2 eggs
finely grated rind of one lemon.

1. Preheat oven to 400°F (200°C).
2. Butter 12 medium-sized muffin cups.
3. Set aside 2 tablespoons sugar.
4. Combine ½ cup sugar, baking powder, salt and flour and mix well.
5. Melt butter in small pan over low heat.
6. Remove butter from heat and cool for 2 minutes.
7. Stir into butter the lemon juice, eggs and rind.
8. Add egg mixture to combined dry ingredients, and stir 12 to 15 times or until everything is thoroughly blended together and moistened.
9. Spoon batter into muffin cups, filling ¾ full, and sprinkle with a little of remaining 2 tablespoons sugar.
10. Place on centre rack of preheated oven and bake for 15 to 20 minutes or until lightly browned.

Orange Oatmeal Muffins

A firm muffin with orange just discernible through the oatmeal flavor.

Makes 12 muffins

1 egg
¼ cup light honey
3 tablespoons melted butter
1 cup milk
1 cup uncooked rolled oats
1 cup whole-wheat flour
1 tablespoon baking powder
½ teaspoon salt
1 tablespoon freshly grated orange peel

1. Preheat oven to 400°F (200°C).
2. In a large bowl, beat together egg, honey and butter until well blended.
3. Add milk and mix thoroughly.
4. Stir in oats. Allow mixture to stand for several minutes.
5. In another large bowl, sift together all remaining dry ingredients.
6. Add dry mixture to milk/oatmeal mixture, along with grated orange peel.
7. Mix just enough to blend. Do not beat.
8. Fill 12 medium-sized muffin cups lined with paper cupcake liner *half* full.
9. Stir batter in bowl gently as you fill cups.
10. Bake on centre shelf in preheated oven for 20 to 25 minutes. Remove from oven when nicely browned.

Peach and Brown Sugar Muffins

Makes a rich, midly spicy muffin treat.

Makes 12 muffins

2 cups all-purpose flour
4 tablespoons brown sugar (firmly packed)
1 tablespoon baking powder
½ cup chopped peaches
    (fresh peeled *or* canned and drained peaches)
¼ teaspoon baking soda
⅛ teaspoon allspice
1 cup commercial sour cream
1 egg
¼ cup melted butter, margarine *or* vegetable oil

1. Preheat oven to 425°F (220°C).
2. Grease 12 large muffin cups.
3. In a large bowl, mix flour, brown sugar and baking powder.
4. Then add peaches, baking soda and allspice. Flour peaches thoroughly.
5. In another bowl, combine sour cream, egg and butter until uniform in color.
6. Add liquid ingredients to dry mixture and stir until moist but lumpy.
7. Spoon into greased muffin cups and bake in preheated oven for 25 minutes.

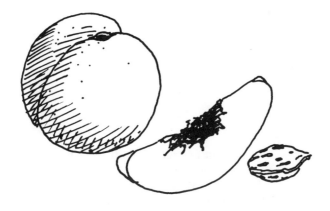

Peach and Cheese Muffins

Makes 12 muffins

1¾ cup all-purpose flour

¼ cup sugar

3 teaspoons baking powder

1 teaspoon grated lemon peel

⅛ teaspoon nutmeg

¼ teaspoon salt

⅓ cup shredded emmenthal (swiss) cheese

⅔ cup milk

¼ cup vegetable oil

1 egg

½ cup peeled and diced peaches
  (1 medium-sized peach should do)

1. Preheat oven to 400°F (200°C).
2. Grease 12 medium-sized muffin cups.
3. In a large bowl, combine flour, sugar, baking powder, lemon peel, nutmeg and salt.
4. Mix above items well, *then* add the shredded emmenthal.
5. In a medium bowl, beat egg for about 1 minute.
6. Add milk and oil to beaten egg and beat again for 1 minute.
7. Stir diced peaches into *dry* ingredients. Be sure peaches are thoroughly floured to prevent settling to the bottom of muffins.
8. Add liquid all at once to the dry mixture, and stir in until well moistened but lumpy. Stir no more than 15 to 20 times.
9. Spoon batter into greased muffin cups, filling ⅔ full.
10. Bake on centre shelf for 20 to 25 minutes in preheated oven.
11. Serve warm.

These muffins can be frozen for future use once cool. When fully cooled, wrap in foil or airtight plastic bags, and freeze. Muffins freeze well for 1-2 months. To prepare for eating, thaw muffins under a layer of foil, in a 400°F (200°C) oven for 10 minutes.

Pear Anise Muffins

An unusual combination — a mixture of pear and licorice essences.

Makes 12 muffins

2 cups all-purpose flour
3 tablespoons sugar
1 tablespoon baking powder
½ teaspoon salt
¾ cup chopped *dried* pears
½ teaspoon grated fresh lemon peel
½ teaspoon anise seed
1 egg
1 cup milk
¼ cup melted butter *or* vegetable oil

1. Preheat oven to 425°F (220°C).
2. Grease 12 muffin cups and pre-sift the flour before measuring.
3. Mix in a large bowl, flour, sugar, baking powder and salt.
4. Add pears, lemon peel and anise seeds to dry mixture and mix again until pears are thoroughly floured.
5. Add egg, milk and melted butter (or oil) and stir well 12 to 15 times so that batter is moist but remains lumpy.
6. Spoon into prepared muffin pan and bake in preheated oven for about 25 minutes.

Carrot Pineapple Muffins

An unusual combination, which tastes a little more like pineapple than carrots.

Makes 24 muffins

1 cup carrot (raw and finely grated by hand)
1 cup sugar
1½ cups all-purpose flour
1 teaspoon cinnamon
1 teaspoon baking powder
½ teaspoon salt
1 teaspoon baking soda
2 eggs
1 teaspoon vanilla extract
½ cup crushed tinned pineapple *with juice*
⅔ cup vegetable oil

1. Preheat oven to 350°F (175°C).
2. Grease well 24 medium muffin cups.
3. Prepare carrots. (If you wish to use an electric blender or food processor instead of hand-grating, be sure to cut carrots into small pieces first.)
4. In a large bowl, mix or sift together dry ingredients except for carrots.
5. To dry mixture add eggs, carrots, vanilla, pineapple and oil.
6. Using *low* motor speed, beat mixture until all ingredients are mixed and moistened.
7. Now beat batter at *medium* speed for another 2 minutes.
8. Using a spoon or rubber spatula, fill muffin cups with batter.
9. Bake in preheated oven for 25 minutes, or until browned.

Note: This recipe produces better results if mixed in an electric blender or eggbeater; hand stirring may yield unsatisfactory muffins.

Carrot Pineapple Muffins with Nuts

High fibre, nutritious muffins with added crunch. Mildly spicy, too!

Makes 12 muffins

2 cups whole-wheat flour
1 cup all-purpose flour
1 cup white sugar
1 teaspoon cinnamon
1 teaspoon baking soda
½ teaspoon salt
4 medium carrots, shredded
2 eggs
1⅓ cups vegetable oil
1 cup chopped nuts
1 cup crushed pineapple, drained
1 teaspoon vanilla extract

1. Preheat oven to 350°F (175°C).
2. Grease 12 large muffin cups, including top of pan.
3. Sift together all flour, sugar, cinnamon, baking soda and salt in a large mixing bowl.
4. Add shredded carrots.
5. In a medium mixing bowl, beat eggs, *then* add oil, nuts, drained pineapple and vanilla. Stir together until well mixed.
6. Combine liquid mix with dry mixture in large bowl, stirring only until moistened but still lumpy.
7. Spoon batter into muffin cups.
8. Bake in preheated oven, on centre shelf, for 35 to 40 minutes.

Cinnamon, Pineapple and Bran Muffins

Dark, slightly spicy muffins for the bran muffin lover looking for something different.

Makes 12 muffins

2 cups whole-wheat flour (sift before measuring)
4 tablespoons sugar
1½ tablespoons baking powder
½ teaspoon baking soda
1 teaspoon salt
2 tablespoons flaked bran *or* whole bran cereal
⅓ cup finely chopped candied pineapple
2 medium eggs *or* 1 extra large egg
2 tablespoons brown sugar
1 tablespoon cinnamon
1 teaspoon vanilla extract
¼ cup melted butter, melted margarine *or* salad oil
1¼ cups milk

1. Preheat oven to 425°F (210°C).
2. Grease 12 large muffin cups.
3. After sifting flour to measure it, re-sift it with *white* sugar, baking powder, baking soda, and salt in a large bowl. If sifting screen has removed the coarse bran from the flour, add back into the bowl.
4. Stir in flaked or whole cereal bran.
5. Mix candied pineapple into flour mixture, stirring it until it is fully coated with flour so it will not sink to bottom of batter.
6. Make a well in this mixture.
7. Break eggs into a medium bowl, and add *brown sugar* and cinnamon.
8. Beat eggs, brown sugar and cinnamon for 1 minute.
9. Add vanilla, butter and milk to other liquid ingredients.
10. Beat liquid mixture another minute.
11. Pour liquid into well in flour mixture.
12. Using large spoon, stir 12 to 15 times, working from centre bottom of bowl outward, until combined and lumpy.
13. Spoon out into greased muffin cups.
14. Bake on centre shelf for 15 to 18 minutes. Best eaten buttered and hot.

Corn Pineapple Muffins

A moist muffin with a strong pineapple flavor. Requires both canned fruit and preserves.

Makes 12 large muffins

2 tablespoons sugar
1 teaspoon salt
1½ cups all-purpose flour
4 teaspoons baking powder
1 cup yellow cornmeal
2 eggs
¼ cup *or* ⅛ pound melted butter or margarine
½ cup crushed pineapple dessert, drained before measuring
1¼ cups milk
1 cup candied pineapple, coarsely chopped

1. Preheat oven to 425°F (220°C). Set shelf in centre of oven.
2. Grease 12 large muffin cups.
3. Sift together sugar, salt, flour and baking soda.
4. Stir cornmeal into other dry ingredients.
5. Beat 2 eggs for 1 minute.
6. Combine beaten eggs with melted butter, drained, crushed pineapple, and milk.
7. Add this mixture to cornmeal/flour mixture.
8. Stir just enough to moisten dry ingredients.
9. Spoon batter into greased muffin cups, filling them ½ full if medium cups, or ⅔ full if small cups.
10. With a spoon, drop chopped, candied pineapple onto top of batter in each muffin cup.
11. Let stand for 10 to 12 minutes.
12. Bake on centre shelf for 20 minutes, or until golden brown.

Note: There is enough batter in the recipe for 36 small muffins. If you make small muffins, reduce baking time by 5-7 minutes.

Pumpkin Muffins (1)

A good recipe for that bit of pumpkin left over from pumpkin pie making.

Makes 12 muffins

1½ cups flour

2 teaspoons baking powder

¾ teaspoon salt

½ cup white sugar

½ teaspoon cinnamon

½ teaspoon nutmeg

¼ cup melted butter

1 egg

½ cup canned *or* cooked and mashed pumpkin

½ cup milk

½ cup seedless raisins

1 tablespoon sugar, to be used at end for topping

1. Preheat oven to 400°F (200°C).
2. Grease 12 medium muffin cups.
3. Sift flour first, then measure out 1½ cups. Mix flour with other dry ingredients, including raisins.
4. Beat egg for about 1 minute.
5. Add melted butter to egg, then add pumpkin and milk. Stir well.
6. Now combine liquid ingredients with flour mixture.
7. Stir only until all dry ingredients are moistened.
8. Spoon into 12 pregreased cups, filling each about ⅔ full.
9. Sprinkle each cup with a little sugar—about ¼ teaspoon, before placing pan in oven.
10. Bake muffins on centre shelf of oven for about 20 minutes, or until golden brown.

Pumpkin Muffins (2)*

If you like pumpkin pie, this recipe will really appeal to you. The amount of cinnamon shown is not absolute, but is just enough to come through.

Makes 12 muffins

2 cups all-purpose flour
½ teaspoon salt
¼ cup sugar
3½ teaspoons baking powder
½ teaspoon nutmeg
1 teaspoon cinnamon
⅔ cup canned pumpkin
1 cup milk
1 egg
¼ cup vegetable oil *or* melted shortening
½ cup finely chopped nuts

1. Preheat oven to 400°F (200°C).
2. Grease 12 medium-sized muffin cups.
3. Sift together flour, salt, sugar, baking powder, nutmeg and cinnamon.
4. Add ⅔ cup canned pumpkin to 1 cup milk and stir together in a large bowl.
5. Add egg and oil to mixture of pumpkin and milk and beat for at least 1 minute.
6. Stir liquid into dry ingredients, and fold in ½ cup of finely chopped nuts.
7. Stir only until all ingredients are combined. Batter should remain lumpy.
8. Fill prepared muffin cups ⅔ full.
9. Bake for about 20 minutes, or until golden brown.

*A Purity recipe, reprinted here with permission.

Spiced Pumpkin Muffins

This is the spiciest of the pumpkin recipes in the book. Don't overdo the ginger!

Makes 12 small or 10 medium muffins

½ cup packed brown sugar

½ cup shortening

1 egg

½ cup canned *or* mashed cooked pumpkin

1½ cups sifted flour

3 teaspoons baking powder

½ teaspoon salt

½teaspoon cinnamon powder

½ teaspoon nutmeg powder

¼ teaspoon ginger powder

¾ cup milk

1. Preheat oven to 375°F (190°C). Grease 12-muffin pan.
2. Cream together sugar and shortening, working it until light and fluffy.
3. Add egg to the mixture and beat.
4. Add pumpkin to mixture and mix again until combined well.
5. Sift together flour, baking powder, salt and spices.
6. Add this dry mixture, alternately with milk to the pumpkin mixture, until all ingredients are stirred in. *Beat well after each addition.*
7. Fill greased muffin cups ⅔ full.
8. Bake on centre shelf for about 25 minutes or until done.

Rhubarb Muffins*

Rhubarb in season is best for these muffins. Use only the stems, never the leaves!

Makes 24 muffins

1½ cups brown sugar

¼ cup salad oil

1 egg

2 teaspoons vanilla extract

1 cup buttermilk

1½ cups finely diced rhubarb

½ cup pecan pieces

2½ cups all-purpose flour

1 teaspoon baking powder

1 teaspoon baking soda

½ teaspoon salt

Topping:

⅓ cup sugar

1½ teaspoon cinnamon

1 tablespoon melted margarine

1. Preheat oven to 400°F (200°C). Grease 24 medium-sized muffin cups.
2. Combine in a large bowl: brown sugar, oil, egg and vanilla.
3. Beat above mixture until well-mixed.
4. Stir into mixture buttermilk, rhubarb and pecans.
5. In another bowl, sift together flour, baking powder, baking soda and salt.
6. Add this mixture all at once to rhubarb mixture and stir until all ingredients are moistened. Do not overmix.
7. Fill prepared muffin pan ¾ full with batter.
8. Quickly combine topping ingredients and sprinkle on top of batter in each muffin cup.
9. Bake in preheated oven on centre shelf for 15 to 20 minutes.

*This recipe is attributed to Bernice Hogan, Smith Falls, Ont. It's a prizewinner.

Chocolate Muffins

Carob (Chocolate), Orange, Date and Nut Muffins

If you love chocolatey things but can't eat chocolate, these carob muffins will satisfy that craving. A recipe for delicious, chewy muffins.

Makes 12 muffins

1½ cups all-purpose flour
½ teaspoon salt (optional)
3 teaspoons baking powder
1 teaspoon baking soda
½ cup flaked cooking bran
½ cup dates, quartered and then chopped
½ cup coarsely chopped walnuts
2 tablespoons carob chips *or* chocolate chips (semi-sweet)
½ cup semi-liquid honey
½ cup milk
½ cup orange juice

1. Preheat oven to 400°F (200°C).
2. Grease 12 large muffin cups.
3. Sift flour, salt, baking powder and baking soda into a large bowl.
4. Stir into mixture, ½ cup cooking bran until evenly combined.
5. Add chopped dates and nuts. Stir them in so they are thoroughly floured.
6. Stir in carob *or* chocolate chips, to flour them thoroughly.
7. In another bowl, combine honey, milk and orange juice. If using semi-solid honey, stir the mixture for 3 to 4 minutes, until honey is more liquified and slips away from edges of the bowl.
8. Combine liquid mixture with flour-date mixture and stir 15 to 20 times or until just combined but still lumpy in texture.
9. Spoon batter into muffin cups.
10. Bake on centre shelf for about 20 minutes.

Note: Eggs, oil and sugar have been intentionally excluded. These muffins do not rise well. They are heavy, crusty, crunchy muffins, chewy with a strong honey taste. Good with butter.

Chocolate, Banana, Raisin and Sunflower-Seed Muffins

A crunchy, fudgy muffin with a decided banana highlight to it.

Makes 18 muffins

2½ cups all-purpose flour
½ cup granulated sugar
4 teaspoons baking powder
¼ cup unsweetened cocoa powder
½ teaspoon salt
⅓ cup raisins
½ cup chocolate chips (semisweet)
¼ cup sunflower seeds (shelled, unsalted)
¼ cup banana chips
1 egg
½ cup vegetable oil *or* melted shortening
1½ cups milk

1. Preheat oven to 400°F (200°C).
2. Grease one 12-muffin pan and 1 six-muffin pan or line with paper liners.
3. Sift together flour, sugar, baking powder, cocoa powder and salt.
4. Stir these ingredients in a large bowl until a uniform shade of brown.
5. Stir in raisins, chocolate chips, sunflower seeds and banana chips, until they are thoroughly floured.
6. Beat together egg, oil and milk for 1 minute.
7. Add liquid mixture to dry mixture and stir 15 to 20 times with rubber spatula.
8. Spoon into muffin pans, filling each ⅔ cup full.
9. Bake on centre shelf for 18 to 20 minutes.
10. Turn muffins onto wire racks, then set right side up to cool.

Chocolate Currant Muffins

These muffins are slightly chewy with a mild chocolate flavor.

Makes 16 muffins

2½ cups all-purpose flour
½ cup white sugar
3½ teaspoons baking powder
½ cup unsweetened cocoa powder
½ teaspoon salt
¾ cup dried currants
1 egg
1½ cups milk
⅓ cup vegetable oil *or* melted shortening

1. Preheat oven to 400°F (200°C).
2. Grease 16 muffin cups (using one 12 cup pan and one 6 cup pan).
3. Place currants in small mixing bowl and cover with hot water from tap. Allow currants to soak for 10 minutes. Then drain them.
4. Sift together in a large bowl, flour, salt, cocoa, baking powder and sugar. If using a sifter, fill it only ⅓ full at a time to keep it from clogging.
5. In a medium mixing bowl, beat together milk, oil and egg for 2 minutes.
6. Add liquid mixture to dry ingredients (including currants) and stir with a spoon 12 to 15 times until fully moistened but still lumpy.
7. With a spoon or rubber spatula, fill greased muffin cups to about ⅔ full.
8. Place both muffin pans on centre shelf of preheated oven. (Fill any unused cups ⅔ full with water. Take care when removing pans from oven that hot water does not spill on your hands).
9. Bake 18 to 20 minutes. Cool on cake racks. Serve with a pat of butter.

Note: If you find these muffins a little too dry, add another ⅛ cup oil to the next batch and serve with a pat of butter on top.

Chocolate, Raisin, Peanut, Graham and Bran Muffins

A mouthful of a title. But what else could you call these muffins?

Makes 12 muffins

¼ cup brown sugar

½ cup shortening

¼ cup molasses

¼ cup unsalted roasted peanuts (if peanuts are salted and still retain jackets, wash and rub briskly to remove jackets)

¼ cup chocolate-covered raisins

1 cup white flour

½ teaspoon salt

3 teaspoons baking powder

¾ cup milk

2 eggs

1 cup Nabisco 100 percent bran cereal

1 cup graham cracker crumbs (medium-fine)

1. Preheat oven to 425°F (220°C).
2. Grease 12 large muffin cups.
3. Cream together brown sugar and shortening.
4. Add molasses, and fold in 4 to 5 times.
5. Stir in peanuts and chocolate-covered raisins.
6. In another bowl, sift together flour, salt and baking powder.
7. Add dry mixture, milk and eggs alternately to creamed sugar and shortening.
8. Fold in bran cereal and graham crumbs.
9. Spoon mixture into muffin cups. (To make muffins lighter, heat greased muffin pan until smoking and then drop batter into cups. Quickly place into preheated oven. Be sure not to handle hot pan without using oven mitts or pot holders, and during this procedure do not set smoking pan onto plastic or wooden tabletop!)
10. If you did *not* follow the smoking pan procedure in step 9, then place filled pan directly into oven at 425°F on centre shelf, and turn setting down immediately to 400°F (200°C).
11. Bake 25 minutes, or until done.

Chocolate Walnut Muffins

These muffins could be described as "round chocolate brownies".

Makes 18 muffins

2½ cups all-purpose flour
½ cup sugar
4 teaspoons baking powder
½ cup unsweetened cocoa powder
½ teaspoon salt
½ cup semisweet chocolate chips (or carob chips)
½ cup finely chopped walnuts (chop first, then measure)
1 egg
1½ cups milk
½ cup vegetable oil *or* melted shortening

1. Grease one 12-muffin pan and one 6-muffin pan.
2. Preheat oven to 400°F (200°C). Place shelf in centre of oven.
3. Sift together flour, sugar, baking powder, cocoa powder and salt.
4. Stir sifted ingredients in a large mixing bowl until thoroughly mixed.
5. Add chocolate (or carob) chips and walnuts, tossing until thoroughly floured.
6. Beat together, in a medium bowl, egg, milk and oil for 1 minute.
7. Add liquid mixture to dry ingredients and stir 15 to 20 times with rubber spatula.
8. Divide mixture between muffin pan cups, filling each ⅔ full.
9. Bake in preheated oven, on centre shelf, for 18 to 20 minutes.
10. Dump muffins onto wire rack, then turn right-side-up to cool.

Crunchy Mocha Muffins

Coffee lovers and chocolate gourmets will appreciate this recipe.

Makes 12 muffins

½ cup milk, warmed

2 teaspoons instant coffee powder

3 teaspoons Nestle Quik® *or* other instant chocolate milk powder

1¾ cups cake and pastry flour

¼ cup flaked bran

1½ teaspoons baking powder

½ teaspoon salt

¼ cup finely chopped walnuts (measured after chopping)

⅓ cup shortening

¾ cup sugar

1 egg

Topping:

½ cup sugar

1 teaspoon cinnamon powder

⅓ cup butter

1. Preheat oven to 350°F (180°C).
2. Grease 12 medium-sized muffin cups.
3. Combine warmed milk and coffee powder with chocolate powder and stir until smooth.
4. Set mixture aside to cool.
5. Sift or stir together flour, bran, baking powder and salt in a large bowl. If using a sifter, check top of screen for any bran trapped above it, and pour bran into the mixture. Stir in walnuts.
6. Cream shortening in a large bowl.
7. Blend into shortening the ¾ cup sugar, beating it until light and fluffy.
8. Now beat egg into creamed sugar/shortening mixture.
9. Add dry ingredients alternately with milk mixture. Make 3 dry and 2 liquid additions *blending well after each* by hand.
10. Fill prepared muffin cups ⅔ full.

11. Mix topping sugar with cinnamon in another small bowl and set aside.

12. Bake muffins in preheated oven for 20 to 25 minutes.

13. Melt ⅓ cup of butter while muffins are baking. (Margarine will also do).

14. When baked, remove muffins from pan immediately and dip muffin tops first in melted butter, then in sugar cinnamon mixture.

15. Serve hot for best flavor.

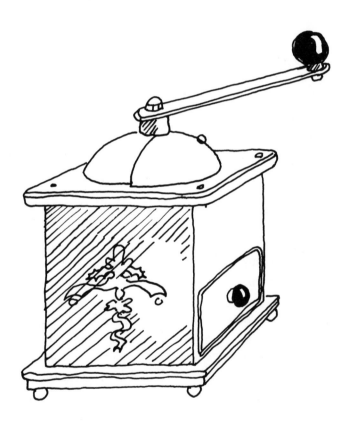

Fennel Chocolate Raisin Muffins

Fennel is a small seed with a licorice-like taste.

Makes 12 muffins

1 cup all-purpose flour
2 teaspoons baking powder
½ teaspoon baking soda
½ teaspoon salt
¾ cup milk
½ cup commercial sour cream
¼ cup vegetable oil
1 egg
1 cup chocolate covered raisins
½ cup brown sugar
1 cup corn flakes cereal, coarsely crushed to crumbs
2 cups Cheerios® cereal, coarsely crushed to crumbs
3 teaspoons fennel seeds
⅛ cup water (warm)

1. Preheat oven to 425°F (220°C) and place shelf at centre level.
2. Grease large 12-muffin pan, including metal surface between cups.
3. Stir together in a large bowl flour, baking powder, baking soda and salt.
4. Set aside above mixture.
5. In a small dish put ⅛ cup water, add fennel seeds and let them soak for ½ hour. Be sure to submerge them.
6. In a medium bowl, put milk, sour cream, oil and egg, and beat with a fork for about 1 minute.
7. Stir in chocolate-covered raisins and brown sugar.
8. In another bowl, stir by hand the corn flakes crumbs and Cheerios® crumbs until uniformly mixed.
9. Add crumbs to milk/sour cream/oil/egg mixture. Let stand for at least 10 minutes so that liquid is absorbed by crumbs. Stir under any dry bits.
10. To above mixture add fennel seeds and any left-over water in which they were soaking. Stir in crumbs/liquid

mixture to distribute them evenly.

11. Add flour, salt/soda/baking powder mixture to liquid mixture and stir with a fork about 15 to 20 times, working flour from centre of bowl in with ingredients from edge of bowl.

12. Using a spoon, pack batter into greased muffin cups, allowing batter to just slightly overflow edge of the cups.

13. Immediately place in preheated oven and bake for 20 to 25 minutes, or until lightly browned.

Note: These muffins do not rise very much. Using more baking powder may help, but occasionally may make them fall apart. Don't be afraid to try a little extra baking powder or baking soda, ½ teaspoon at a time, to gauge the effect.

Allow these muffins to cool for about ½ hour before removing them from the muffin pans.

Rice, Corn Flour, Date, Chocolate and Poppy Seed Muffins

Don't try to memorize this title — you're sure to forget something!

Makes 12 muffins

1 cup corn flour (*not* cornmeal)
½ teaspoon salt
3 tablespoons cocoa powder
½ cup loosely packed brown sugar
½ cup cooked rice
1½cups cake and pastry flour
⅓ cup poppy seeds
1 cup coarsely chopped dates
3 teaspoons baking powder
1 egg
1¼ cups milk
⅓ cup vegetable oil *or* melted margarine

1. Preheat oven to 400°F (200°C).
2. Grease 12 large muffin cups.
3. In a large bowl, mix together corn flour, salt, cocoa, sugar, cooked rice, cake flour, poppy seeds, chopped dates, and baking powder.
4. Beat together egg, milk and oil in a medium bowl.
5. Stir liquid mixture into dry mixture until lumpy. Do not overstir — just moisten all ingredients.
6. Fill muffin cups ⅔ full.
7. Bake on centre shelf of preheated oven for 20 to 25 minutes.

Rum, Fruit and Chocolate Muffins

This recipe was formulated to convert the rum-ball lover to muffin-eating.

Makes 12 muffins

1 cup mixed candied fruit and citrus peel and raisins, in any combination
⅓ cup dark rum
1¾ cups all-purpose flour
¾ teaspoon salt
3 teaspoons double-acting baking powder
2 eggs, well-beaten
1 cup milk
3 tablespoons unsweetened cocoa powder
¾ cup sugar
4 tablespoons melted butter

1. Marinate fruit, peels and raisins in rum for 48 hours.
2. When fruit has soaked for two days, preheat oven to 400°F (200°C).
3. Grease 12 large muffin cups, including tops of pans.
4. Mix together chopped mixed fruit (and any excess rum left in bowl) with 2 tablespoons of the flour in a large bowl.
5. In a medium bowl, sift together remaining flour, salt and baking powder.
6. In a medium bowl, beat eggs first, *then* add milk, cocoa powder, sugar and butter and beat again for 2 minutes. Mixture should be foamy. Check bottom of bowl to be sure that all chocolate powder is dissolved. If not, stir cocoa from bottom and beat some more.
7. Mix fruit with dry ingredients in large bowl, stirring until floured. This will prevent fruit from settling to bottom of muffins.
8. All at once, add liquid mixture to dry ingredients, then stir 15 to 20 times from centre outward until combined but lumpy.
9. Spoon into muffin pans, almost to top.
10. Bake in preheated oven for 15 to 20 minutes.
11. Allow to cool in pans before trying to remove these muffins.

Note: You may use paper muffin cup liners for easier removal. If you plan to keep these muffins beyond the day you make them, store them in an airtight container to keep them moist.

Nut Muffins

Christmas Cake Muffins

If you like light Christmas cake, chewy, nutty, fruity and rum flavored, you will love this recipe.

Makes 12 muffins

¼ cup shredded coconut (sweetened *or* unsweetened)

1 cup chopped mixed candied fruit, consisting predominantly of red and green cherries

⅓ cup dark rum (*or* ¼ cup vodka *or* liquor store alcohol plus one 2-fluid ounce bottle of rum extract, mixed together)

½ cup raisins

2 cups *plus* ¼ cup all-purpose flour
  (keep aside extra ¼ cup)

½ cup sugar

1 teaspoon salt

4 teaspoon baking powder

⅓ cup coarsely chopped walnuts

1 egg

⅓ cup vegetable oil *or* melted shortening

1 cup milk

1. 24 hours before you plan to bake muffins, soak coconut and mixed fruit in rum in an airtight container to prevent evaporation of alcohol.
2. After 12 hours, shake container to redistribute fruit in alcohol, and to be sure that it is all marinated. Some of the raisins may also be added to mixture at 12 hour stage, particularly if there sems to be an excess of rum in the container.
3. After 24 hours prepare to make muffins by preheating oven to 400°F (200°C). Set shelf in centre of oven.
4. Grease 12 medium muffin cups, or place paper liners in bottom of pans. Grease top flat edges of pan, between cups, as overflow of batter will stick otherwise.
5. Sift together 2 cups flour (keeping aside remaining ¼ cup), with sugar, salt and baking powder.
6. Stir in nuts and raisins.
7. Spoon macerated fruit into flour mixture using a slotted spoon so that excess rum drains off. Be sure all fruit is

thoroughly coated with flour, or it will settle to bottom of muffins. If you wish to add some color, save ⅓ cup of fruit for topping later.

8. Add remaining rum from marinade container to egg, oil and milk, in a medium bowl, then beat for 2 minutes.

9. Stir liquid mixture into dry ingredients until blended but still lumpy. All ingredients should be moistened.

10. If the batter has an excess of unabsorbed liquid around the edge of the bowl, stir in the remaining ¼ cup of flour which was set aside for this purpose. If this is not enough, add *a little* more. (Too much flour will turn these muffins into rum-flavored, fruit filled bricks! So use as little flour as you can get by with, to soak up excess liquid).

11. Spoon into prepared muffin cups, filling to the top or even to overflowing.

12. If you saved some of the fruit for topping, press a little of it into the top of each lump of batter now, with a spoon.

13. Bake in preheated oven for 20 minutes.

14. Allow to cool for 5 or 6 minutes before attempting to re-move muffins from cups.

These muffins are best served hot, with 5 minutes of removal from oven, topped with a pat of butter. The rum flavor is at its strongest when fresh from the oven and gradually decreases in potency over a couple of days (if these muffins last that long!).

You will find that they are light, fine-textured and very fruity in flavor. If you use a large proportion of citrus peel, the muffins will have an agreeable lemony tang to them.

Maple Poppy-Seed Muffins

A crunchy, irresistible muffin with a strong maple flavor. Delicious hot!

Makes 12 muffins

2 tablespoons butter, softened to room temperature.
¾ cup sugar
4 teaspoon maple extract
2 eggs
½ cup poppy seeds
1 cup commercial sour cream
1 tablespoon dark molasses
¼ cup milk
2¼ cups all-purpose flour
1 teaspoon salt
2 teaspoons double-acting baking powder
½ teaspoon baking soda

1. Preheat oven to 425°F (220°C).
2. Grease 12 large muffin cups.
3. In a large bowl, cream together butter and sugar.
4. Stir in maple extract. Mix until uniform in color.
5. Add two eggs, and stir until thoroughly combined.
6. Stir in poppy seeds. Allow mixture to stand for 5 to 10 minutes to let seeds absorb moisture.
7. Stir in sour cream, molasses and milk.
8. In a medium bowl, sift together flour, salt, baking powder and baking soda.
9. Stir dry mixture into bowl containing liquid ingredients. Batter will be quite heavy. Stir 15 to 20 times, or until all dry ingredients are just moistened. Do not overstir.
10. Spoon batter into prepared muffin cups. *Batter will slightly overfill cups.* It will not overflow as it is quite stiff. (The batter will probably not drop from the spoon without an assist from your fingertips.)
11. Place pan on centre shelf and bake for 25 minutes.
12. Allow muffins to cool for 5 minutes in pan, after removal from oven.

13. Remove from pan and let muffins cool on wire racks, or serve immediately while still warm, split open and with a pat of butter melting over each half muffin.

Maple Walnut Muffins

Not quite as strong-tasting as maple-walnut ice cream, but the *artificial flavoring* can be increased if desired. Do not increase the maple syrup or you will upset the liquid balance of this recipe.

Makes 12 muffins

1 cup all-purpose flour
¾ cup whole-wheat flour
1 tablespoon baking powder
1 teaspoon salt
¼ teaspoon cinnamon
½ cup chopped walnuts
   (*Note:* Set aside some nuts for topping, if used)
½ cup butter
⅓ cup maple syrup
⅔ cup milk
1 egg
½ teaspoon vanilla *or* maple extract

See notes below for optional topping.

1. Preheat oven to 425°F (220°C).
2. Grease 12 regular muffin cups.
3. In a large mixing bowl, combine all dry ingredients except nuts.
4. Melt butter over low heat.
5. Add maple syrup and milk to butter and stir.
6. Beat in egg and vanilla (or maple) flavoring.
7. Stir butter mixture into dry ingredients.
8. When liquid and dry ingredients are well blended, stir in walnuts.
9. Spoon batter evenly into muffin cups, leaving room in each one for topping. If topping not used, bake immediately.
10. If topping is to be used, combine:
      3 tablespoons sugar
      ¼ teaspoon cinnamon
      3 tablespoons finely chopped walnuts
11. Blend topping ingredients well and sprinkle over each uncooked muffin.
12. Bake in preheated oven for 15 to 20 minutes. After removing, allow to stand at least 5 minutes before removing muffins from cups.

Pecan Muffins

Related to pecan pie, though not quite as sweet.

Makes 12 muffins

2 eggs
½ cup flour
1 cup brown sugar
¼ teaspoon baking powder
⅓ teaspoon salt
1 cup pecans

1. Preheat oven to 400°F (200°C).
2. Grease 12 medium muffin or cupcake tins.
3. Combine all ingredients and stir just until moistened —
   lumps will remain in batter.
4. Fill muffin cups ¾ full and bake in preheated oven for
   10 minutes.

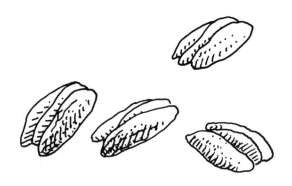

* Reprinted with permission from the
Rochester Hadassah Cookbook;
Helen Hecker, editor.
Submitted by Eve Mendelson.

Pecan Almond Muffins

The pecans and almonds give these muffins a memorable flavor.

Makes 12 muffins

2 cups all-purpose flour
2 teaspoons baking powder
½ teaspoon salt
1 cup lightly packed brown sugar
¾ cup blanched almond halves or slivered almonds
½ cup pecan halves
2 eggs
1 cup milk
¼ cup vegetable oil *or* 3 tablespoons melted shortening
½ teaspoon almond extract (optional)

1. Preheat oven to 400°F (200°C).
2. Grease 12 medium-sized muffin cups.
3. In a large bowl, mix together flour, baking powder, salt, sugar, pecans and almonds. Be sure nuts are thoroughly floured.
4. In another bowl, combine eggs, milk, oil and almond extract, and beat for 1 minute.
5. Stir liquid ingredients into dry mixture until batter is just moist but still lumpy.
6. Spoon batter into greased pan and bake on centre shelf in preheated oven for 20 minutes, or until lightly browned.
7. Allow to cool for a few minutes in pan, then remove and place on wire racks to cool completely.

Pecan Date Muffins

Another one for the pecan connoisseur, with dates added for chewiness and body.

Makes 12 to 16 muffins

2 eggs
½ teaspoon vanilla extract
⅔ cup flour (sifted before measuring)
1 cup white *or* firmly packed brown sugar
1 teaspoon baking powder
⅓ teaspoon salt
¾ cup *each* finely chopped dates and pecans

1. Preheat oven to 400°F (200°C).
2. Grease 12 large or 16 small muffin cups.
3. Re-sift flour with baking powder and salt in a medium bowl.
4. In a large bowl, combine eggs with sugar and vanilla.
5. Stir flour mixture into egg mixture, stirring no more than 5 to 10 times.
6. Add dates and nuts, and continue stirring until well-mixed (10 more times maximum).
7. Spoon batter into buttered muffin pans.
8. Bake in preheated oven: if small cups are used, bake 10 to 12 minutes.
   If large cups are used, bake 18 to 22 minutes.

Sweet Potato, Pecan Muffins

An unusual recipe for the pecan lover.

Makes 9 large or 18 small muffins

1½ cups all-purpose flour
¾ teaspoon salt
3 teaspoons baking powder
¼ cup butter
3 tablespoons brown sugar
½ cup pecans, coarsely chopped
1 cup cooked and mashed sweet potatoes (yams)
2 egg yolks
¼ cup *(or more)* milk
2 egg whites
mixture of cinnamon and sugar: 5 parts white sugar to 1 part cinnamon

1. Preheat oven to 375°F (190°C).
2. Grease 9 large or 18 small muffin cups.
3. Sift together flour, salt and baking powder.
4. Cream together butter and light brown sugar.
5. Add pecans to dry mixture, and stir in to flour them well.
6. Mix cooked, mashed sweet potatoes into 2 egg yolks.
7. Add milk to mixture of egg yolks and potatoes and stir.
8. Combine dry ingredients mixture with liquid to make batter.
9. Stiffly beat egg whites, then fold into batter. (This provides extra lightness in the muffins.)
10. Spoon into prepared muffin pans.
11. Sprinkle tops with a little of the cinnamon sugar mixture.
12. Bake for about 35 minutes on centre shelf.

Note: If using a muffin tin with 12 large holes or cups, partially fill 3 empty holes with water before baking.

Toasted Hazelnut Muffins

Toasted hazelnuts have a strong but not overpowering nutty taste. You can use ¾ cup if you want to increase the flavor and crunchiness.

Makes 12 muffins

½ cup prepared hazelnuts, finely chopped
  (also known as filberts)
2 cups all-purpose flour
3 tablespoons sugar
½ teaspoon salt
1 tablespoon baking powder
1 egg
¼ cup melted butter, shortening *or* vegetable oil
1 cup milk

1. Toast hazelnuts as follows:
   - Preheat oven to 350°F (175°C).
   - Arrange nuts in a single layer on cookie sheet or shallow baking pan. Leave space between nuts.
   - Place cookie sheet on centre shelf and bake for 15 to 20 minutes.
   - Occasionally, open oven and using oven mitts or potholders shake cookie sheet lightly to expose all surfaces to air.
   - Remove nuts from oven and allow to cool for a couple of minutes.
   - Rub off as much of the dry brown skins as possible.
   - Chop nuts on a cutting board. Chop as fine as possible. You may also use a coffee mill, but do not turn the nuts into flour!
2. Sift together flour, sugar, salt and baking powder in a large bowl.
3. Stir in finely chopped nuts. Increase oven temperature to 425°F (220°C).
4. Beat egg with butter and milk, in a medium-sized bowl. Grease 12 large muffin cups.
5. Make a well in centre of flour mixture and pour liquid mixture into well all at once.

6. Stir batter until all ingredients are just moistened, but still lumpy.

7. Spoon batter into prepared muffin cups and bake in pre-heated oven for 20 to 25 minutes or until well browned.

If you wish to add an easy topping, save a little of the chopped nuts and mix 3 tablespoons nuts with 1 tablespoon sugar. Sprinkle this mixture onto the muffin batter in each cup just before baking.

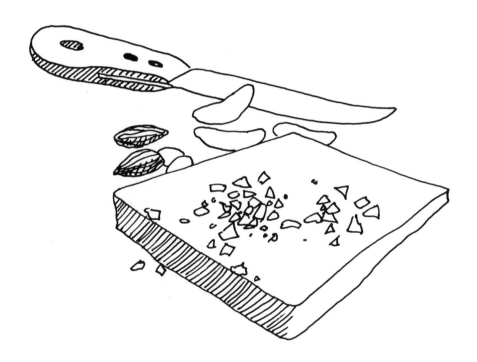

Walnut/Black Currant Muffins

While these muffins call for black currants, dark raisins can be readily substituted. The nuts make the muffins a little chewy.

Makes 12 to 14 muffins

1 cup all-purpose flour
3 teaspoons baking powder
½ teaspoon baking soda
½ teaspoon salt
¼ cup lightly packed brown sugar
1 cup whole bran
1 cup black currants *or* raisins (or half of each)
¼ cup quartered walnuts
1 egg
1 cup milk
¼ cup liquid honey
¼ cup vegetable oil *or* melted shortening

1. Preheat oven to 400°F (200°C).
2. Grease 12 large or 14 medium-sized muffin cups.
3. Sift together flour, baking powder, baking soda, sugar and salt in a large bowl.
4. Stir in currants *and/or* raisins, to flour them thoroughly. Stir in walnuts.
5. In a medium bowl, mix together bran, egg, milk, honey and oil.
6. Stir liquid mixture into dry ingredients only until combined.
7. Fill greased muffin cups ⅔ full.
8. Bake on centre shelf for 20 to 25 minutes.

Black Cherry Yogurt/Walnut Muffins

Commercial black cherry yogurt usually has added artificial flavor which gives these muffins an extra-strong cherry taste. Try to obtain yogurt that has chunks of black cherries, rather than the pureed type, as the chunks give a burst of flavor.

Makes 12 muffins

3 eggs (*or* 2 large duck eggs)
2 tablespoons soft butter or margarine
¾ cup sugar
½ cup chopped walnuts
1 cup commercial black cherry yogurt
2 cups all-purpose flour
2 teaspoons bran
½ teaspoon baking soda
2 teaspoons baking powder
½ teaspoon salt

1. Preheat oven to 425°F (220°C) and grease 12 muffin cups.
2. Cream together in a large bowl, eggs, butter and sugar.
3. Add walnuts and yogurt, and stir 5 times.
4. In a medium bowl, sift together flour, baking soda, salt and baking powder.
5. Add bran and stir lightly to distribute it through the flour.
6. Add flour/bran mixture to yogurt/egg/sugar mixture.
7. Stir until mixed but lumpy, a maximum of 20 times. Ingredients should be moist but not smooth.
8. Spoon batter into prepared muffin pan and bake in preheated oven for 20 minutes.

Note: No additional sugar is required if the commercial yogurt is very sweet, as it usually is. If the black cherry yogurt is not sweet, add an additional ¼ cup of sugar (maximum) to the yogurt/sugar mixture, if you like. More sugar than this, however, will ruin the recipe.